300

THE ENEMIES OF LOVE

THE ENEMIES OF LOVE

by
DOM AELRED WATKIN
Monk of Downside Abbey

LONDON
BURNS & OATES

PERMISSV SVPERIORVM O.S.B.

———————————

NIHIL OBSTAT: ANDREAS MOORE, L.C.L.
CENSOR DEPVTATVS
IMPRIMATVR: E. MORROGH BERNARD
VICARIVS GENERALIS
WESTMONASTERII: DIE XIII MARTII MCMLVIII

MADE AND PRINTED IN GREAT BRITAIN AT
THE CHAPEL RIVER PRESS, ANDOVER, HANTS,
FOR BURNS OATES & WASHBOURNE, LTD.,
28, ASHLEY PLACE, LONDON, S.W.I

CONTENTS

FOREWORD

THE short introduction found below will, I trust, make clear the purpose of these pages; in a sentence, I have first tried to show that human love (if rightly understood) is divine love translated into the terms of human experience, then to examine the assaults which selfishness makes upon that love and, finally, to indicate where and how they may be overcome.

I make no apology for the subject. Experience, particularly where the young are concerned, shows that every love of the human heart contains a challenge and an invitation, that each such love—even if in the end frustrated, as far as this world is concerned—can be of lasting value in teaching the individual to overcome selfishness and thus to prepare himself for the loves of later life. It is in the conviction that so many marriages become frustrating or unhappy precisely because husband and wife have never really learned what it is to love or how to cope with love's problems, that in these pages I have urged that no love should be allowed to run to waste, that each is valuable, if rightly used, and that to learn to love is the truest and noblest education.

Not all these pages have been written with the young particularly in mind. The first six sections deal mainly with emotional love—of whatever kind; the last two are concerned with all the varying forms of human affection, though emotional love is not, of course, excluded.

If this little book can bring some comfort, courage or hope to any for whom love brings more pain than happiness, I should feel greatly rewarded. In the words of the Roman Missal: *profero, Domine, . . . suspiria iuvennum.*

I

INTRODUCTION

" IF I shall be lifted up, I shall draw all things to myself," said our Lord, speaking of the new life to be given to men by his redemption. " All things "—every faculty of man, every form of human experience, everything that man does and is, save sin alone, is drawn into Christ and into his life. Apart from sin there is nothing that cannot partake in and be an expression of the eternal life of Christ endlessly renewing itself in time and place by the sacraments of his presence.

" This is the bread that gives life to the world." And what is the life? It is his life: " I live, now not I, but Christ lives in me." Without Christ there can be no life; without him all human endeavours must perish in that death which took its origin in human sin, without him all human hopes are but shadows lengthening towards darkness, desires which can never attain enduring fulfilment. But with him and in him, all human endeavours become sacraments of life, pledges of eternal glory, hopes that can never be confounded. In very truth all things have been drawn to Christ, and in him have found their meaning, their fulfilment and their purpose.

We have, then, but two categories of experience. On the one hand, there is selfishness and sin which uses all that is in itself lovely and good as food upon which to feed; on the other, we have the life of grace which concerns itself not with what it can receive or extract from persons and things, but with what it can give, spending itself in carrying out the work of Christ in the world. To repeat: there are but two categories of experience—life and death, love and selfishness, giving and grasping, grace and sin.

We emphasize this at the very start because any discussion upon love tends to be confused by the introduction of a third factor ; only too often we find ourselves speaking as if the world of nature—the world of everyday human experience—existed as a kind of *tertium quid* in the battle between grace and sin. At first sight, indeed, this is what it appears to be, but if we reflect more deeply we shall see that, though the world of nature provides the battle-ground, it cannot itself become a combatant. If, for example, as we say speaking loosely, " we have sinned by being led away from God by natural beauty ", it is not natural beauty that has led us away from God, it is we who have misused natural beauty by employing it to feed our own self-indulgence. For us it is tainted because we have poisoned it; in itself, however, it is what it always was, a loving creation of God and fair because it reflects Beauty itself. Indeed, because all in itself is holy and sin misuses and perverts holy things, all sin must partake in some measure of the nature of sacrilege.

As there are not three categories of experience, equally there are not three loves: charity, something wholly supernatural; natural love, something merely emotional or biological; and lust, something entirely turned to self-indulgence. There are but two loves—the love of Christ which seeks to give itself to God and to men,

and the love (if we may call it so) of self which tends to
use men, and even God if it could, to feed self-indulgence
and selfishness. These are the two lives, the two cities,
of St. Augustine: the *Amor Dei usque ad contemptum sui*
and the *Amor sui usque ad contemptum Dei*. For the
Christian, love is the love of Christ or it is not love.[1]

Love: perhaps the most common word upon our lips
and, yet, what a multitude of different significances it
has! It can mean the love of God, the love of parents,
the love of children, the love of brother and sister and,
perhaps most vivid in the order of experience, that
emotional love which drives us powerfully towards one
or other of our fellow beings. Nevertheless all these
loves are but different expressions of one and the same
love, " the love of God poured forth into our hearts by
the Spirit living in us ".

It follows, then, that no experience of the human
heart in love can lie outside the ambit of Christ's love
and life. It is selfishness alone which, remaining mute
and unresponsive to the impulses of Christ's life in men,
at first implicitly and then directly denies love and finally
extinguishes it. " The wages of sin is death." We
cannot, therefore, too often make clear that all love, as
love, is a reflection of the love of that heart of Christ in
which our own hearts live.

Our religion thus reaches down to the roots of ordinary
human experience and is intimately concerned with what
we think, with what we feel and with what we are, for
it is here that the battle is joined between love and
selfishness and between fulfilment and frustration. It is

[1] These five paragraphs are quoted, with the permission of the
Editor, from an article by the present writer in *The Life of the
Spirit*.

here that God reveals himself to us and transforms into significance and transmutes into eternal value what would otherwise be but a disconnected series of passing episodes and a pattern of shifting shadows. It is here that we find God; that, in virtue of our sacramental union with him, we work with him in redeeming the world and ourselves. It is in ordinary human experience, the stuff of which life is made, that the work of the Incarnation is continued and made manifest in us.

The most vivid, and frequently the most painful and baffling, experience of human life is that of a love in which the emotions are powerfully affected, " romantic love " as it is sometimes and rather unhappily called. Emotional or romantic love, particularly that of early youth with its wild elations, its sudden despairs, its easy fruitions that so quickly may turn to frustration, its pangs of jealousy, its sense of insecurity, its uneasy restlessness and, at the same time, with its spontaneity, its generous idealism and its vivid sense of opening windows upon a fresh and more wonderful world—can we have here something with which religion, the life of Christ, is not concerned?

Do not let us try to evade the problems of emotional love. To those who have never been in its toils, or who have almost forgotten the feelings of earlier days, it may seem that such a subject has little scope for the spiritual writer and few attractions to the casual reader. This would perhaps be true if such emotional love be viewed solely from the angle of a calm maturity; but such a maturity is something that has to be acquired and, if it is to be other than mere negation, it is something that has had to be fought for. Meanwhile, are we to say that those who have passed through the battle should remain mere indifferent spectators of those still in the thick of it?

" But ", the reader may ask, " though it is quite true that many, if not most, people go through these painful experiences at one time or other, why bring them out into the cold light of day? Surely they are usually but of transient importance, part of the inevitable process of ' finding onself ' which we all have to go through? " Such questions would be unanswerable were it our intention to describe the phenomena of emotional love in order to pander to a morbid interest, or if our object were but to give a few practical hints upon the necessity for self-command and the importance of not committing follies whose memory will be merely a source of embarrassment. Such, however, is not our intention. What we are hoping to do is to show that an experience of the most searching and almost universal character is one from which, not only much good may be derived, but which, if rightly used, may be one of the greatest and most formative influences for good in human life. We wish to show that, in the response to the situation presented by emotional love, there is the real possibility of learning how to love God and man; that, here as in every other circumstance presented to us by the direct or permissive will of God, there is a situation which calls for co-operation with him in the fullest possible way.

Again, though many books have been written dealing admirably with the problems of sexual temptation or with the metaphysics of love, there is little which attempts to handle the practical problems raised by emotional love for those who are trying to serve God and attain Christian perfection. Sexual sin and temptation, though often very difficult in practice to meet, do not as a rule assume the complexity and subtlety of the difficulties raised by the pleasures and pangs of emotional love. Indeed, those caught in the toils of these difficulties find it hard to know where to turn for help and advice. Contemporaries usually have little valuable assistance to give other than their sympathy, while those who are more mature tend to forget the all-sifting character of the experience and thus to brush aside its problems with breezy exhortations urging the participants " to pull themselves together ". Though many have benefited enormously by wise and sympathetic advice in the confessional, such advice must of its nature tend to be empirical and to work from situation to situation. What we have tried to do here is to treat the matter more generally, to see what situations are to be expected and to suggest how best to meet them. Above all, we have endeavoured never to separate human love from the love of God, which is charity, and in which alone can human love find its meaning, expression and fulfilment.

II

WHAT IS LOVE?

THERE is only one love, that perfect, personified, love of the Father for the Son and of the Son for the Father which we call the Holy Ghost. Love alive. Love a person. Love, the total and utter giving to each other of the Persons in the Godhead in a mutual abandonment which " the heart of man cannot conceive ".

But this love is by no means merely a distant and remote pattern for the loves of feeble humanity; by our incorporation into Christ at Baptism and our union with him in Holy Communion, that love becomes at root our own and our own reflects Love itself. Human love, therefore, is not extinguished in God's love, but is fulfilled and made sure, certain and fruitful.

By Baptism, as we have said, our natural human life is incorporated into the life of Christ, the divine life of the Trinity. We live in Christ and Christ lives in us, and, thus living in and by Christ, we live in and by his love, " the love of Christ poured forth into our hearts by his Spirit dwelling in us ". This state of love into which we are plunged by Baptism is increased by the other sacraments: it is rekindled in Confession, nourished by Holy Communion and stimulated into action by Confirmation, while the grace of Matrimony makes the love of husband and wife a particular expression of the very love of Christ himself.

2

Such, then, is the fundamental character of love, such is the love that is given to us by our incorporation into Christ. But what of love as a human experience? What of the numerous expressions of human love? What of this divine love in what might be described as its phenomenal aspect (for here we are dealing with divine love translated into terms of human experience)?

" It is not good for man to be alone ", and one of the deepest urges of human nature is to love and to be loved. To love—to give onself to other persons; to be loved—to be chosen by others as the especial object of their affection and interest. By ourselves we are insufficient, hesitant, unable to express what we mean, what we are. We have the urge to communicate ourselves, to become the objects of solicitude, of interest and of understanding. We want to be valued, not for our qualities, but for what we are. We feel we have something to give, if only there is someone to receive with gratitude what we so long to communicate. In the difficulties and vicissitudes of human life we long for a refuge, a place of peace, the security which love alone can give. Tremulous on the verge of self-expression, tongue-tied with ineffable longings, haunted by the feeling that some great and transcendent experience lies just around the corner if only we can find it, wearied by the inevitable sameness of daily experience, the human heart thirsts for love, for the means of self-expression which love alone can in some measure provide. It is this thirst, this *Sehnsucht*, which lies at the depths of most human strivings. Ambition may disguise it, forthrightness may conceal it, intense activity temporarily may smother it, passion may strive to substitute itself for it, but in the depths of the human heart that longing remains. It is one of the deepest things in our nature; for the thirst is the thirst for God—" let him who thirsts come to me and drink ".

" How can a man love God whom he cannot see, if he does not love man whom he can see? " Human love is the expression of the love of God working through the natural, God-created, instincts of humanity. There is the instinct by which parents love their children and children their parents, the instinct by which brothers and sisters love each other, the instinct, perhaps more of the mind than of the body, which creates friendships founded on a community of interests, an appreciation of quality or a pleasure and joy in another personality. Finally, and usually strongest of all, there is the mating or sexual instinct, drawing men and women together in a natural urge to participate in the work of God's creation and making that creation (like the creation of the world) the work of love. All have these instincts. Some are stronger and some weaker, some are more apparent in one person than in another. At one time in life one may be strong and the others almost unrealized, and then a shift of consciousness or the simple passage of time will bring about a change, and new urges will to some extent take the place of the old. We should perhaps say in passing that this is not a text-book of psychology; it is not our purpose to assert or to refute the now popular notion that all human love is of its nature sexual in character. From the practical point of view such a notion, even if true or partly true, is of little significance to us; our task is to deal with love as experienced.

Here, I think, we shall find a broad distinction in human love which may be of value to our discussion.

Love seems mainly to fall into two distinct categories: love that we have, so to say, already found ourselves with, and love that is the result of our own deliberate choice. It is not always easy to make this distinction, and we shall have more to say about it later, but for the present it will be enough to distinguish between the love which takes its roots in the family, the love that we are born with as it were, and the love which results from our own choice of friends of either sex. It is in the second category that, as a rule, what we call emotional love is found.

Emotional love takes its origin in the senses, and displays its presence through feelings which become more or less vivid and absorbing according to character and circumstances. It may never be expressed, sometimes it is not even recognized for what it is, but it presents a challenge to the whole personality. It is our response to this challenge which is one of the most important elements in human life; for the emotion itself is not love, it can be the pathway to it or it can be the road to its rejection. Love itself lies deeper than feeling and further than desire, for the love of God which is drawing all men to himself and to each other may be translated into feeling, but cannot be confined by it.

Let us then, at the start, beware of confusing love itself with feeling or expression. Emotions, feelings, desires are not themselves love (despite the popular usage of the word); they are God-given urges to enable man to translate love into action. Their purpose is to provide the incentive to love's expression in human behaviour. They stimulate the response to the voice of Christ saying: " Give and it shall be given unto you ".

" Give ", that is the operative word; it is in this word that we may perhaps find the clue to love's complexities. To go back to where we were before: the Father gives himself utterly to the Son, the Son gives himself utterly to the Father, this abyss of giving and receiving is the love of God, the Holy Ghost. The Word was made flesh, the Son of God became man, and, as man, poured himself out in love for the Father and in love for all those whom the Father loves. He loved the Father and us " even unto death ". Loving and giving are, then, identical in God and must, therefore, at root be identical in those depths of the human spirit where men live by the life of God and love with his love.

It is here that love has, as it were, a head-on collision with human sin. In the depths of his being man is one with Christ, but this divine life has to work through that fallen nature which humanity has inherited from Adam. The effects of original sin require no demonstration, they are only too apparent in the daily experience of human life. A profound disintegration exists in man. In the depths of his heart he wishes to give himself to God and to others, but his fundamental will is impeded by a tendency which works in precisely the opposite direction, that tendency which we call selfishness.

Love wishes to give, selfishness desires to receive. Love reaches out to others, selfishness reaches from others to ourselves. Love values others for themselves, selfishness values them for ourselves. Love has the confidence and peace which proceeds from the certainty that it has all to gain and nothing to lose, selfishness exists in a state of precariousness, knowing that it is attempting the acquisition of something that can never be securely or permanently gained. Love knows that each human personality in Christ is of infinite value, selfishness, at least half consciously, is aware that no human intimacy can satisfy its insatiable appetite.

Love and selfishness: it is here that the battle is fought, the contest gained or lost. Love wishes to give itself, but is hindered by a thousand selfish impulses which disguise themselves only too completely under new and unexpected forms. Weakness seems to be more apparent than strength. Resolution tends to falter and perseverance seems but to be the pursuit of the unattainable. Hurt and bruised in the contest, the heart longs to say to itself, " Never again ", and the abandonment of love seems a desirable and a sweet release. Indeed, to the superficial, love is but the source of pain, the mainspring of jealousy, the pursuit of insecurity and the cause of restlessness and frustration. Some have even appeared to hint that the love of God and the love of men are in some measure opposed; that the former leads to peace and the mortification of human desire, while the latter is the pursuit of self-indulgence at the expense of the love of God.

Love, however, is the occasion, not the cause, of pain. The cause of pain is our selfish nature which tries always, and often in the most subtle manner, to arrest the course of love and to pervert the urge to give into an appetite to receive. It is true that without love there can be no pain, but it is equally true that without love there can be no happiness, for there can be no life. The dead can no longer shiver in winter's cold or burn in the noonday sun, but suicide is no response to human miseries, it is merely the stark admission of defeat.

Granting, then, that love means the urge to give and the impulse to dedication, and that selfishness is the desire to use persons and things to obtain self-satisfaction, we have now to pass on to a further but very necessary distinction. At once the question will present itself: " Do you mean to say that the desire to receive love has no part to play in love's perfection, that all hope of being loved should be abandoned? " And the answer, of course, is clearly " No ". How, then, are we to distinguish between selfishness and a perfectly proper desire that our love should be reciprocated?

We shall try to see the full answer to this question later on, but for the moment we shall merely point out that though love itself always remains the same—pure and perfect giving—for its full fruition it requires reciprocation. To love totally and not to be loved in this world is love in its fundamental form; to love and to be loved is love in its full fruition. As always, the love of God sets the pattern for all loves. The Holy Ghost is the mutual love of the Father and Son, love wholly given and completely received. Our own love of God is the giving back to him of what we have received; " we love him because he has first loved us " as the apostle puts it. The ideal of human love is a complete giving and a complete receiving; to be loved is as much an urge of the human heart as to love.

Our interrogator will, however, at once put a further question: " But, surely, we are here back to selfishness again, is it not precisely from this desire to be loved that our selfishness springs? " If this were indeed so we should have to relinquish all desire for human love, and the deepest urges of the human heart would have to be thwarted if such a desire could not reflect the love of God. Moreover, if this were so, there would be no need for our present discussion. We have, rather, to remember two vitally important considerations.

The first of these is that to love *in order* to be loved is not love. The essential character of love is to exist and to act beyond the consideration of return: if we love *in order* to be loved we are not loving God or a human being for themselves but for ourselves. Our motive is not another but ourself. This does not mean that we may not hope for our love to be returned or that we may not long for reciprocation, but it does mean that our love precedes and exists beyond the hope of return. It means that our love is not called into being by such a hope (in the case of God we already possess his love), nor does its intensity increase or decrease with the response which it receives. In fact, if we look closer, we shall see that it is circumstances which determine the response to love, that these circumstances are the revelation of the will of God, and the revealed will of God is nothing more or less than the particular path of love in our regard chosen for us by divine providence.

This brings us on to our second consideration: it is circumstances that must dictate the nature of the love to be given and the character of the love to be received. Human life is made up of an immense variety of different relationships, different calls to love. There is the natural love in the family into which we are born; there is the love that must spring from vocation in life, like the love of the priest for his people or of the master or mistress for his or her pupils; finally, there is the love of pre-dilection or choice where the emotions are usually engaged. It is obvious that there are situations in life when circumstances can make emotional love an occasion of sin; thus a married man may not form attachments of a kind that would have been perfectly right and proper in the days before marriage. It is all these varying circumstances which provide the clue to the distinction between selfishness in the desire to be loved in a particular way and a perfectly legitimate wish for love's return. We must love, really love, all; but in each case the character of our love and the form in which affection is given and returned must be different. It is by responding completely to these situations that true love is shown. There are circumstances when we can give ourselves totally and may rightly hope for a total response to our love; there are other circumstances when our love ought to be given with no thought whatever to the response we may be given. In all circumstances the character of the response, its fittingness and rightness, must depend upon all the complex web of times, persons, places and situations through which God reveals to us the path our love must follow. Therefore, granted the presence of the desire to be loved, it is God's will alone, revealed through persons and events, which can show us whether the fulfilment of that desire for response is for us, in the given situation, a pledge of love or an impulse to self-indulgence.

Love has as many, or has even more, enemies than truth, for, necessarily involving the highest faculties of man and being the most intimate expression of the life of Christ within him, it wounds mortally the selfishness springing from fallen nature. Emotion can so easily get out of hand, the judgment can so easily become warped and physical desire can so quickly draw all before it. Yet, as the apostle says, " the love of Christ impels us "; we cannot by-pass love or its problems. To love properly is not only to achieve fulfilment and satisfaction in this world, to be able to give to others what is of unique and inestimable value—oneself, but it is also to set one's feet upon the path to holiness. If we do not learn how to love in this world, we shall have to learn it in that painful refining of love that we call purgatory. " I chose you and I set you that you might bear fruit and that your fruit should endure ", said our Lord. The fruit of the Tree of Life is love and it is through love that we also come to fruition. Love is life and to love is to learn to live.

We may now pass on to a consideration of the experience of love in human life. In the following four sections it is our purpose mainly to deal with emotional love and its problems, for these problems are usually the most immediate and urgent, especially for the young; and they are problems which are by their nature more subtle and difficult to meet than almost anything else in ordinary human experience. It must be confessed that we are treading on difficult and delicate ground, for we are trying to put into words what is almost ineffable. Nevertheless, it is surely useful to attempt to discuss the manner in which emotional love can be the expression of the love of Christ. How many marriages would have been saved from disaster if both parties had gone into them with a real understanding of the nature of love and of its joys and difficulties. Such disasters are only too frequently due to the mishandling of earlier loves in life. Each love is a challenge to selfishness, and if this challenge is met and overcome, each love leaves the participants in a better situation to deal with the next. The love may not have come to anything, circumstances of character or time or temperament may have proved too much for its fulfilment, but it has not been, if rightly used, a waste. Something of selfishness and self-indulgence in the individual will have been killed, and he or she will be a better person from it and in a better position to love those others for whom divine providence is preparing him or her.

III

THE AWARENESS OF LOVE

(NOTE: In the following two sections we shall employ two mythical characters—Hilary and Vivian—to illustrate what we are trying to say. These names have especially been chosen as they are the christian names equally of men and women. This should enable the reader to apply them to all possible circumstances in which emotional love can exist. Unfortunately English has no personal pronoun expressing " he or she " and therefore it has sometimes been necessary to reiterate the names of Hilary and Vivian where a pronoun would grammatically have been more correct.)

WHO can record the various stages of love's dawning or describe the subtle process by which liking and interest become love and affection? Yet, as an experience, it is part of the history of every life. To begin with, there is the first awakening of love—perhaps even in young childhood—when a new and exciting element seems to have been introduced into human life. It is the moment when the unquestioned likings and affection of earlier years take on a new character and are accompanied by new feelings; the moment when the individual realizes that he or she is beginning to love in quite a new way. It may be a long time before the new state has forced itself upon the attention, before the participant has understood what has happened, and yet it is a point of no return. A fresh element, now translated for the first time into real experience, has come into life, and nothing can ever be quite the same again. For the first time the word " love ", long read of in books and long talked of in conversation, has a real meaning and significance; the individual now feels that he or she is living on a new plane of experience, has moved on, as it were, into a new dimension.

Almost equally mysterious are the first awakenings of all subsequent human loves. Hilary may know Vivian for years, may have talked to Vivian for hours on end on any subject under the sun, may have played tennis or bridge with Vivian on frequent occasions, and all this without any particular thought of the future of their relationship and with an utter unselfconsciousness with regard to its nature. Then, perhaps imperceptibly, there is a subtle change, at first of an almost trifling character, but a change which is a symbol of something fresh and new, just as the mere grating of the weather-vane may show that the wind is blowing from a fresh point of the compass. Something has happened; a small thing, a mere incident, perhaps a sudden awareness of the quality of a voice, of the expression of an eye or of the outlines of a profile against the light, perhaps the new intimacy of an unexpected confidence or a shared secret, and from thenceforth the feelings of Hilary for Vivian enter upon a fresh stage and take on a completely fresh character.

What is it that has happened? What is the cause and nature of this new awareness and heightened interest? Why has Vivian taken on an entirely new and absorbing significance for Hilary? How, in fact, are we to analyse the experience? It is perhaps in the question of significance that we may find the clue. It is not that Vivian's qualities have changed or that Vivian's appearance has altered, but these qualities and this appearance have become significant to Hilary precisely because they are Vivian's. It is not that anything about Vivian has changed, or in itself necessarily noticed for the first time; it is that Vivian's appearance, way of talking or even mode of thought are now objects of interest and fascination because they are the expression of Vivian. In fact what has taken place is a new awareness of the personality of another.

This awareness begins of course in the senses. It is through the senses alone that mankind can communicate and express itself, and it is obvious that biological and psychological urges play an important part in this natural attraction. But we cannot stop there. Experience shows that not every human being who is, even superlatively, attractive (as we say) does in fact attract us. There are many with few natural attractions for whom deep love is felt. If we stop short merely on the level of the senses we stop short of the answer to our question. We have merely described the mechanics of the impulse to love, we have not analysed the impulse itself. We shall have to look deeper.

Each human person has been individually created by God and created uniquely for a unique relationship with him. This unique character of the human personality means that each human being exists as something without parallel in creation, each man (as a person) has never existed before, can never exist again, can never be duplicated. He need fear in the depths of his personality no competition from anyone. Man's gifts and attributes, whether of intellect, character or looks, have to face the open market of the world, but his personality, the innermost recesses of his being, remains outside the barter of a world's traffic.

Personality is unique. It can never, therefore, be expressed in terms of anything else. It cannot even, as can character, be understood by analogy or comparison. It must therefore remain in one sense inexpressible, incapable of being defined by human words and concepts and impossible to be described in rational terms. The knowledge which we can easily gain *about* people lies helpless before the completely different knowledge that is implied when we feel that we *know* people.[1] No amount of knowing about people will make us know them. In the one case we are dealing with their attributes, in the other with themselves. The mystery of what we mean when we say: " I am I ", " he is he " or " she is she " is something before which words fail and for the understanding of which human experience alone can be our guide.

Our Lord said " I shall call my sheep by name ", and in saying this he condescended to that profound instinct in human nature which wishes to give each person a special name, something which distinguishes him or her from others, something which emphasizes the special character of human personality, something which expresses the human desire to manifest an awareness of this uniqueness. It is this instinct which lies behind the use of nicknames, of the pet names often given by parents to their children, of the superficially foolish

[1] Of course we are here employing the words in their strict, not their casual, sense.

31

names sometimes coined by lovers for those whom they love. It is this instinct, on a higher level, which the Church employs in giving a special name to the newly baptized and confirmed: " I shall give them a hidden food and a new name ", said the prophet, and these new names are signs of God's special and individual election, of his unique relationship with each soul. A name is, therefore, one of the symbols by which we express personality, and when we speak of the " name of the Father and of the Son and of the Holy Ghost " we are expressing in symbolic form the triple personality of God which lies at the heart of all reality and all existence.

God loves each person with an infinite love; he created man for love of him, his Son died for man's love and he has given his very own love, the Holy Ghost, to be his life by grace. God can neither deceive nor be deceived; the human personality as the object of God's infinite love must, inasmuch as a created being can, be infinitely lovable. When God asks us to love our neighbour as ourselves and when St. John tells us that the love of our neighbour whom we can see is the witness of our love of God whom we cannot see, we are not being asked to take up some kind of attitude or to try to pretend for the purpose of pleasing God that our neighbour is a worthy object of our love. In loving our neighbour we are putting ourselves in tune with fact, with the fact that our neighbour is infinitely worthy of our love. We are not asserting that his qualities, his ideas, his ways of thought or action are lovable, we are saying that *he* is. Again we have arrived back at human personality, existing beyond all the phenomena of human behaviour and the concealments of human appearances.

Sometimes, however, it is given to us to penetrate beyond the veil of thought and action and to reach out directly to the personality of another by a kind of insight. It is true that it is usually the senses that have put us on the road, but the final insight is something which the senses of themselves cannot give. Through this insight we have attained to a direct, if incomprehensible, knowledge of the personality of another; and, because that personality is infinitely lovable, we have almost no choice but to love it. Lovers have had a glimpse of something that draws them beyond the realm of considerations and the jog-trot of arguments. Hilary has loved Vivian because Hilary has seen Vivian for the first time as Vivian really is. In a very true sense Hilary has seen Vivian as God sees Vivian.

It is this truth that lies below all the phenomena of loving and of falling in love. As we have seen, biological and psychological considerations have played their part in leading to a state of love, but they do not form the constituents of it, they cannot of themselves create it. They can but lead towards, or away from, an insight which is far higher than themselves; an insight of the unique nature of another's personality. And that personality, being infinitely lovable, draws love to itself.

The accompaniments of human personality—character, disposition, habits, thoughts, appearance, gestures—now become significant to the lover, not primarily on their own account but because they are seen as an expression of the true self, really but obscurely known, less obscurely loved. Love is not, therefore, some kind of irrational passion, but flows from an insight beyond the scope of the discursive reason. It does not blind; rather, it is

3

dazzled by its own light. It is an insight into persons as they really are. " This is my rest for ever and ever, here will I dwell because I have chosen it ", says God speaking in the psalms of the created soul and personality of each man born into the world. It is for this rest that love yearns. It is from this parentage that love is born.

IV

THE GROWTH OF LOVE

PROVIDED that there is a chance of reciprocation, the period of time during which love grows and intimacy increases is usually one of comparatively little difficulty. It is a time of discovery, when each meeting means a heightened intimacy and when each hesitancy overcome is a fresh and glorious conquest. It is like an expedition into a new world where fresh wonders reveal themselves on each day's journey, and each wonder is welcomed as a pledge of greater wonders to come.

This is the great time of action. Meetings are arranged, conversations prolonged, common interests sought for. Confidences are given and received, each one more delightfully intimate than the preceding. Letters are written at great length and with great care, and letters are received which are perused again and again in order to extract the last ounce of affection from the written page. Presents are exchanged and birthdays and festivals are eagerly looked forward to, and on these occasions the postman is awaited with a happy anxiety. Fresh modes of displaying the growth of affection are pondered, and perhaps executed with a self-congratulatory sense of achievement. Little symbols of intimacy are envisaged and proposed—some special smile or gesture perhaps—to be something shared as a secret by both

35

parties. Indeed, even for the indolent, it is now a time of action: no period is too long to be spent on this all-absorbing voyage of discovery, no distance too great to be traversed at love's behest.

If love be reciprocated, as we are now supposing it to be, sooner or later a climax is reached. Hilary confesses love for Vivian and Vivian makes it clear that the love is returned. Hilary can now say: " I love and I am loved ". It is the apparent climax of love's growth.[1]

All appears to be so simple now. Everything seems to have fallen into place. Not only are Hilary and Vivian of deep significance to each other, but everything else seems significant too. All has now a meaning. There is almost as much meaning in the hideous as in the naturally beautiful; in the soot-stained privet by the ash-heap in the back garden as in the sun slanting through the beechwood, in the sullen drip of November rains on the gleaming city pavement as in the wild daffodils nodding their heads in a stiff breeze of March. Little unpretentious houses glow warm and domestic; the cinder path by the railway line is a royal road to adventure.

People have far more meaning too. Despite what can be said about lovers' selfishness, at this stage of love home affections are treasured as never before, and, in general, the boring become interesting, the inarticulate eloquent and the surly merely reserved. Mechanical sounds, even, participate in this renaissance: the noise of the train on the rails, the hooting of the distant tug

---

[1] We have selected this moment to describe the climax of which we speak, but it is obvious that in many cases it may come later on, e.g. shortly after marriage.

in the estuary, the hum of bicycle wheels on a damp road—all these are echoes of a song of triumph.

In short, the meaning of life seems to be for the first time really understood. Old fears and inhibitions are now thought to be things of the past, a new confidence and assurance appears to have been gained and a new insight into human life to have been acquired. The future seems to stretch out full of promise, invitingly beckoning those who love and are loved along the road to a rich fulfilment. All difficulties now seem easy of solution, all perplexities now simple to resolve and all doubts now at an end. For the rest of human life the lover and the loved will so walk on for ever, as it were, in the sunshine of an English countryside.

This period of growth which culminates in the admission of reciprocated affection is, as we have said, the period when love presents least problems. Difficulties of course there may be, but they are as nothing to the difficulties which lie just round the corner, for there can be no doubt at all that the moment when those who love each other think that all problems have been solved and all doubts laid to rest is the very moment when the real difficulties make themselves felt. What has seemed to be so simple, so sure, so easy and so permanent will soon be revealed for what it is—an earnest of sureness and permanence and an invitation to it, but by no means its possession. There is much to be suffered and much to be learned before the full possession can be enjoyed in peace.

Later on we shall be looking at some of the difficulties which lie in the path of love and at some of the threats to its possession which have yet to be met; but, for the

moment, let us try to see why this first climax (if we
may so call it) of human love, with its apparently complete
and permanent victory, is something very precariously
won and with difficulty maintained. In short, let us ask
ourselves why this climax is little more than a step on
the road; an important and necessary step, but still no
more than a step.

Coelum non animum mutant qui trans mare currunt,
said the poet of old, and we may render this very roughly
as " Those who cross the sea change their surroundings
but not themselves ". It is soon found that the possession
of a love which seems to have transmuted everything
does not lead at once or easily to an alteration of disposition or character. Circumstances have, in fact, for
a time almost conspired to hide this truth and lovers are
only too easily prone to say to themselves: " I am not
the same person that I was six months ago ". In a way
this is true: a new vision, a fresh insight, undiscovered
potentialities have made themselves apparent; but,
deeper down, the old self remains to test the strength
and scope of the new experience.

In the first place, there have as a rule been few difficulties to surmount. Doubtless there have been moments
of impatience and jealousy and times when selfishness
has had to be resisted, yet so far there has been no serious
challenge to love. In general, all has gone easily and
resolutions have remained up to the present for the most
part untested.

Again, all that has happened up to the present has
had the note of novelty. It has been a time of discovery
when both parties have been reaching forward to a new
experience, a greater intimacy, a future that lies ahead.

38

They have been discovering more about each other, and each meeting has been in its way a new and thrilling experience. It has been like living in a new dimension.

This atmosphere of seeking, finding, discovering and attaining is bound to give an appearance of almost effortless facility to the pursuit of love. Achievement, if sometimes slow, seems to be almost inevitable; self-sacrifice is comparatively easy under the circumstances, patience is seldom tested and possessiveness is as yet hardly a temptation. The almost inevitable tendency to build up a romantic picture of the character of the loved one has not up to the present had to stand up to the hard light of day. Dreams of the future have not yet had to be translated into terms of actual life and living.

It is for all these reasons that the moment when love has been acknowledged and returned is so often a turning-point in love's experience. Though all seems now so simple and inevitable and the future so full of promise, yet the impulses which have brought about the present situation have now to change their character and meet new challenges. The time of difficulties is coming and the chief period of discovery is over. There is no longer that urge to conquer which gives such dynamic force to love's search, for in one sense (the sense most immediately apparent to the feelings) the quest is over and the impetus which it has given has now spent itself. An entirely fresh situation has now to be faced.

Indeed, it is just at this time when all difficulties seem to be over that they appear on every side. And what makes them harder to cope with, or even to recognize, is that as a rule they are entirely unexpected; they seem, as it were, to come out of a clear sky. Beforehand all was sunlight and life promised to be one long summer of such days, and now, without warning, the sun appears to have " gone in " and great storm-clouds lie overhead. And all this without warning or presage; it has almost the alarming impersonality of some utterly unrehearsed calamity of nature.

The fact is that many of the illusions with which love is wont to clothe itself now reveal themselves for the first time for what they are. Hilary begins to discover defects in his or her own character of which until now he or she had largely been ignorant. Hilary feels impatient, even critical, of Vivian (earlier on how impossible this would have seemed); Hilary feels pangs of jealousy without basis in reason or fact; Hilary begins to discover that love is not the panacea to every evil of human life and that temptations and even sins, laid aside or neutralized under love's impulse, are underneath as active as ever.

Moreover, Hilary now begins to notice defects in Vivian which beforehand were either completely unobserved, or, if noticed, regarded as pleasing weaknesses. Hilary begins to wonder whether it is a stolid conventionality rather than an impenetrable depth of character that lies behind those dark eyes of Vivian's. Hilary begins to find certain of Vivian's irrational prejudices slightly annoying, certain habitual gestures of emphasis irritating. Occasionally there is a *timbre* in Vivian's voice that grates on Hilary's ear. Hilary sometimes wonders whether Vivian always tells the truth.

The meetings between them are as eagerly looked forward to as ever they were, but too frequently something comes up to cloud their perfect happiness.

Perhaps Vivian arrives late and makes no adequate apology to Hilary, and Hilary thinks: " I have been waiting all day for this meeting, I have thought about it ever since I got up and yet it obviously doesn't mean much to Vivian who hasn't even bothered to be on time ". Vivian, who is by nature vague, was, in fact, every bit as eager as Hilary; but Vivian is not in the habit of noticing times and places very accurately, still less of apologizing for being late. And so Hilary tends to sulk and is inclined to be uncommunicative and to talk in monosyllables until some gesture of affection causes moodiness to be forgotten.

Or, perhaps, Vivian is annoyed because Hilary will insist upon talking about a recent performance of Gluck's *Orpheus* and appears to be paying little attention to Vivian's detailed description of the semi-finals of the local tennis tournament. Vivian begins to wonder how far Hilary really cares; only a month ago Hilary would have listened with breathless eagerness to anything Vivian cared to say. And usually, sooner or later, jealousy is felt by one or both. There was the matter of the letter which Hilary refused to read aloud, there was Vivian's picnic in Epping Forest about which a strange reticence was maintained, there was the friend at whom Hilary smiled but who was not introduced to Vivian. More clouds come between them; more explanations are needed and are given; another reconciliation follows.

We could multiply almost endlessly a list of such incidents, such difficulties in the path of love; but there is no necessity, for human experience will provide more than enough examples of what we are trying to say.

All we are attempting to do is to illustrate the fact that, when things seem to be at their easiest and the course of love the most smooth, a point has been reached in which the genuineness, stability and unselfishness of love are being tested. In fact, selfishness is beginning to war with love and grace with sin and the victory is not to be gained in a moment. Up to the present selfishness has largely been disguised and it is now beginning to make itself apparent.

In a word, the testing-time which seems to come in almost all human endeavours has now arrived. The initial emotion is now turning to something deeper but less felt, and in consequence all the forces that war against love seem to be rallying their strength. Love, as yet almost untested and untried, has to strike deeper roots into the rock of reality; and, at first, the rock seems hard and incapable of providing nourishment.

These are precious but painful times when the inevitable lesson is being learned that in this limited world, and with the sin of Adam reflected in fallen human nature, love cannot exist without suffering. The reason is not far to seek and we have only to repeat what we have said above: love, being the love of Christ in our hearts, wishes to give and selfishness values everything by what it can receive. It is this conflict between love and selfishness which is the cause of the suffering which all real love must undergo, until, purified and refined by pain, the lover finds that love itself is its own reward and giving is the only pathway to fulfilment.

Yet, with what difficulty is this truth experienced. Selfishness is aided by the inadequate control of emotion and passion which is the lot of fallen man; it is supplemented by the sense of inadequacy which is the *damnosa hereditas* of the human race and which makes men forever seek for reassurance about themselves from what can never reassure; it is aided by the almost inexhaustible capacity of the human mind for delusion about itself and about others; it is ministered to by the power of the imagination in constructing situations and indulging in dreams against which reality seems drab and unsatisfying.

The situation is made even more difficult from the fact that the loved one is as prone to selfishness as the lover, and it is only too easy for selfishness to call to selfishness and self-indulgence to self-indulgence. Further, the whole atmosphere of modern thinking about love tends to obscure the issue: to most contemporary minds love is something that " happens ", some transcendent experience to which lovers are passive, the times and moments of which are outside their control. Such " love " is usually peddled in the cinema or on the television as a somewhat inconsistent mixture of simple physical attraction and a dream-like ecstasy not of this world. This is not necessarily to criticize " romance " or " glamour ", for they can have a valid meaning as the interpretation of a genuine experience—the falsity does not mainly lie there, it lies in the unexpressed notion that love has its rules and experiences which lie beyond the powers of the human will, and that any fading of love is a fact of nature beyond human control or foresight.

All love—real love—is a challenge. It invites a head-on collision with selfishness and an abandonment of self-seeking the extent of which time alone can show. Love presents the soul that is trying to seek God with a situation which has to be met by every weapon that can be used. In this battle " to love and to be loved " does not mark the completion of a finished edifice, it merely provides the raw materials from which the edifice can be constructed. The success of love has to be fought for, selfishness has to be fought against; patience, hope and conviction are all needed, perseverance and courage at all costs must not fail.

Let us face up, then, fairly and squarely, to the difficulties that lie ahead; but do not let us, at the same time, be forgetful of the assets we possess, the weapons with which we are armed. To begin with, if the love be in accordance with what is right and suitable, it must in its essence be a reflection of the love of God, a love which, like faith, " can conquer kingdoms ", a love which in itself " knows no change nor shadow of alteration ". God is therefore on the side of love; his mother, " the mother of holy hope ", is helping with her intercession; the numberless saints who have experienced the battle in which love is now engaged are aiding with their prayers.

The Church, too, is at hand with her sacraments. There is Penance to heal the wounds received in the strife, there is Confirmation by which the Spirit of Love is poured into our hearts to enable selfishness to be burned up in the " fire of his love ", and for those for whom complete physical unity is the right end of human love, there is Matrimony by which human love and its expression are consecrated and hallowed.

Lovers have been given that precious insight into the personality of another which lies at the heart of human love and which transcends all its expressions and, thus, the urge of the human heart to give itself lies below the perhaps more apparent presence of selfishness.

Lovers do not, then, go into battle unarmed. They have all the weapons which must, if they will to use them, bring inevitable victory either in this world or in the next. They should not therefore be put off by the sense of their own inadequacy, by their record of past self-indulgence or by fears for the future. As long as human love is an expression and reflection of Love itself, it must in the long run emerge triumphant and victorious.

V

THE ENEMIES OF LOVE

I. ANXIETY AND A SENSE OF INSECURITY

ONE of the commonest poses which we all tend to adopt at one time or another is that of being completely self-sufficient. We like to pride ourselves upon " standing upon our own feet ", we like to imagine that our happiness does not depend upon anyone or anything, that the love and interest of other people, though pleasing to us, are in no way necessary for our happiness. We can even in some measure persuade ourselves that we really do enjoy such an independence, and it is certainly not very difficult to persuade others that we do.

What, however, is the reality underneath all this undaunted exterior? We are shrinking, defenceless, easily hurt and very dependent upon others. Indeed, there is a deep sense of insecurity in the human spirit, a fundamental lack of self-confidence. We need the sympathy, the affection, of others to fill the void which reaches down so deeply in us. This point needs little elaboration, for, whatever we may pretend to in public, whatever we may like to pose as to ourselves, its truth is only too apparent. How easily we are hurt by criticism, how deeply our self-confidence is wounded by mis-understanding, how often we ponder in secret upon the effect of our words and actions upon others and wonder why we did this or said that, ending up either by hoping anxiously that all will be forgotten, or inventing to ourselves plausible reasons to prove the wisdom of our actions or words.

We have a whole wardrobe of disguises which we employ to hide this insufficiency from others, a whole timber-yard full of scaffolding to prop up our self-confidence. It would be impossible to list them all. A forthright manner hides an inner hesitancy, ambition seeks a position to give a status, an impatience with demonstrative affection conceals the desire for it, reticence is often but disguised shyness, a pretended indifference hides the pains of extreme sensitiveness. In short, we all tend to have our own ways of disguising the insecurity which we all feel.

The causes of this insecurity are doubtless complex, but, fundamentally, they must take their origin from the fact that God is the sole ultimate reality, the sole real security in our lives, and that any part of human life and experience which does not live by him and with him is not vivified by his life and must therefore be precarious. Apart from God, it is apart from reality; and, shore up and buttress it as we may, deep down within ourselves we know its fundamental insecurity. Apart from God we have " no abiding city " and the root cause of human insecurity is to be found in the ravages made by human sin, our own and that of Adam, in human nature.

But other factors increase this sense of insecurity. The very fact that others share it makes our own greater, for it is the nature of this insecurity to try to achieve stability by carving out for itself some real or imagined niche in life. And this inevitably means that others must try to expand at our expense. It is almost a law of human life that the simple trust of the small child soon turns into the wary suspicion of the growing boy or girl. Openness gives place to shyness, simple self-revelation to reticence. The old simple confidence goes (it may be regained later on, but not in its original simplicity) and men tend to become self-contained islands and find it hard to bridge the waters which separate one boxed-in self-consciousness from another.

This sense of insecurity may easily become an enemy of that giving of oneself that is love. It may first appear in the comparatively innocuous form of anxious self-questionings: " Why did I say this ? " " Why didn't I seize this opportunity ? " " If only I could recall that letter from the post! " But these minor difficulties are not usually of great importance. The sense of achievement which the growth of love gives can impart a temporary self-confidence which can easily overcome such minor anxieties. Insecurity usually becomes far more of a factor in love's problems at a later stage, the stage in which love has been given and received.

Fundamentally, it makes itself felt in a doubt as to the strength with which love is reciprocated or if it be reciprocated at all. Incidents occur which seem to strike a blow at love's self-confidence—a missed appointment, a reticence, with its sense of something withheld, or an apparent coldness of manner. Such incidents are at once translated by insecurity into its own terms: " Does Vivian really love me ? " is Hilary's anxious self-questioning. " How do I know that Hilary is as fond of me as I am of Hilary ? " ponders Vivian.

It may seem to be a small doubt, springing from a

small incident, but equally it may be a turning-point which marks the beginning of love's solid growth or signalizes its decay. It is natural, and indeed almost inevitable, that this sense of insecurity should be felt; in itself it is of little importance, what is important and vital for the future is the nature of the steps taken to gain and to retain the sense of confidence and security. Or to put it in the concrete, " What are Hilary and Vivian to do ? "

It will probably be easier if we begin with the answer to the question: " What should Hilary and Vivian not do ? " Faced by such a sense of insecurity, with a doubt as to whether love be returned, natural human instinct seems to cry out for a tangible reassurance. Doubt, that instinct feels, can be allayed by what it may term a " proof " of affection—a smile, a word, a gesture, an explanation—all, or any, of these can form the matter for this tangible " proof ". Insecurity or doubt, therefore, seeks to be healed by a tangible proof of affection. Such is the natural urge of human nature; and yet experience shows that this method of coping is every bit as precarious as the insecurity which it is supposed to allay. If the tangible " proof " be not given, the sense of insecurity deepens into one of positive frustration and restless suspicion; while, on the other hand, if it be given the effect is extremely short-lived. On any given occasion a " proof " of affection may overcome the doubts of lovers, but it will soon be discovered that before very long these doubts will come back to demand, in their turn, yet another " proof " of affection. There will, then, be a tendency to alternate between fits of elation, in which love appears to be possessed for ever, and depths of despondency when doubt darkens the whole spirit. Each " proof " of affection will need to be stronger and probably more explicit than the previous one, and usually it is at this point that the other enemies of love will make their appearance: jealousy will add torment to insecurity and possessiveness will spring from the constant demands for tangible reassurance.

In short, tangible reassurance will not provide what it seeks, for there is no such thing as a tangible " proof " of love's presence. Experience soon shows that expressions of human love, valuable as they are as signs of a love already firmly rooted and established, cannot of themselves fully assure the doubtful. The human sense of unsureness is too profound to be permanently overcome by any tangible expression of feeling; the reason can only too easily construct considerations to nullify its value, the imagination can conjure up chimaeras of every kind which will render them nugatory, while words and gestures must lose much of the immediacy of their impact with the passage of time. What Hilary and Vivian must not do is to try to turn external expressions of affection into means of reassurance about each other or into " proofs " of love's presence.

" Give and it shall be given unto you ", said our Lord, and this applies to the whole of human experience, and in particular to the experience of human love. Love implies giving and its fruition and continuance must depend upon giving, not indeed without hope of return, but without consideration of return. Love must give itself beyond all tangible proofs of return, beyond all considerations whatsoever. The other person must be loved for himself or for herself, not for what he or she can give. Love must strive to give itself totally. Until this fundamental act of self-renunciation has been made, love must remain precarious, for its continuance will depend upon such factors as states of mind, thoughts of return, demonstrations of affection, all or any of which may fail at any moment.

To be strong, weakness must be admitted. It is the humble who are exalted, and to be humble means to come to terms with the fact that fallen nature in itself is utterly vulnerable and weak, though, in and with God, it can do all things. Insecurity and lack of confidence must first be fully and freely admitted, their presence should be no occasion for surprise or alarm. This admitted, and keeping in mind that a sense of insecurity in love cannot be met by tangible " proofs " of affection, we find that the only answer to love's problems is to love more. Thus, in reply to our original question, " What are Hilary and Vivian to do ? ", we must answer that both must strive to give themselves to each other irrespective of the response they may or may not receive. It is only in this forgetfulness of self, this direct onslaught on selfishness, that security in love may be found. To limit or to qualify love by its real or imagined response is to sin against its very nature and eventually to destroy it.

It may be felt that this doctrine is hard and, indeed, almost impracticable, but it will be found not only to be possible but, in the end, to be necessary. That it is hard is very true; love, however, is not something that just " happens ", it is something that has to be made— indeed, we use the phrase " making love " and no description could be more exact. It is true that love, being the giving of self and the overcoming of selfishness, must at times be not only painful but difficult: there is the latent selfishness of two persons to be overcome, there is the urge for quick and easy solutions of all difficulties, there is the feeling—derived in part from modern notions of " romance "—that such difficulties ought not to be; all this means that the building up of love is a long and arduous task, a process of self-refinement, a slow growth, an acquired habit of self-renunciation.

Such a picture may well seem to be at first sight an alarming one. It should, however, be remembered that to give onself completely is one of the most profound instincts of the human heart, far deeper than the folds and folds of self-love which enwrap it. In loving we are following our deepest instincts. Moreover, the feelings of happiness which are attached to human love make the difficult path far more easy and God has given them to attract men along the road. Further, deep down, the lover knows the value of it all and that the suffering undergone to gain and to retain the love of another is as nothing to the fulfilment to be found there. Finally, any human love which is rightly directed may be sure of the grace and help of God, who is not only the author of all love but is love itself. The consciousness of this will do much to give comfort in the dark hours of suffering which are inevitable for the attainment of love's growth and perfection.

Paradoxically enough, although insecurity may at times become more apparent in the pursuit of love, yet it is love which does more than anything else to overcome it. The love and affection of others, the knowledge that they value us and see us as we really are, more than all things builds up confidence. Not a false confidence based on human achievements, status, importance in the eyes of the world, or upon a sense of the possession of charm, wit, intellect or beauty, but a real confidence based upon a real fact, the fact that in ourselves, in the depths of our personality, we are infinitely worth while. The knowledge that another sees us as we really are with that insight into personality which love gives, and that, seeing us as we really are, loves us for it, can overcome our sense of insecurity as nothing else can. Conversely, when we try to give ourselves to another and to cast aside our selfish preoccupation with ourselves, we are enabled to overcome the hesitancy and precariousness which that self-preoccupation must induce. In this, as in every problem of human life, love supplies the answer.

2. JEALOUSY

Jealousy is perhaps the most universal of human passions and far more of life's decisions and judgments are motivated by jealousy than most people would care to admit. The desire to find fault with the rising and the successful, the grudging acquiescence in praise given to another, the irritation felt when others gain advantages in which we do not share, the secret hopes that projects about which we have not been consulted will come to disaster—in all these and in many other ways jealousy seems to penetrate even into our inmost thoughts.

That jealousy is one of the most powerful enemies of love is obvious enough, for, if a sense of insecurity presents a difficulty, jealousy will almost inevitably make itself felt. Jealousy, in fact, is a direct consequence of this sense of insecurity. It is but one step from the doubt that Hilary has of the presence and strength of Vivian's love to a jealous feeling that there is another whom Vivian loves more. The sense of insecurity, in one way rational enough in itself, has been irrationally transferred to a doubt of Vivian's love—irrationally because Hilary has no real evidence that Vivian's attitude is in any way changed. Irrationality now goes a stage further by the attempt of Hilary to rationalize it: Hilary has to form to himself or herself some reasonable explanation of the unreasonable feeling of doubt and therefore the mind posits the presence of a rival. This may sound a complex explanation of a simple state of mind, but it is usually true.

Hilary and Vivian, however, do not usually realize quite what is happening. For them it is commonly a matter of some small and unforeseen incident which suddenly clouds the sunshine and security of love. The sight of Vivian smiling at some third person may perhaps send Hilary into a turmoil of jealousy and anxiety; a half-heard conversation or a carefully concealed letter may fill Vivian with jealous curiosity. So irrational can jealousy be, that it may even be felt for incidents in Hilary's past which are now long over and almost forgotten. Indeed, there is no end to the occasions which may cause jealousy, no bounds to the possibilities of its appearance and there are no precautions that can totally overcome all occasions of it. Two persons are concerned, both prone to it, and in the heightened sensibility of love such irrational emotions are bound to try to make themselves felt. Though some persons are by nature more jealous than others, there are few who are totally free from its promptings. Jealousy, therefore, proves itself to be a persistent and dangerous enemy of love.

The temptation, then, is almost inevitable; how is it to be met? As before, there is a right and a wrong way of coping with it; one which reflects the first instincts of selfishness, the other which is the real path to love.

Selfishness employs two main weapons to deal with jealousy. Not realizing the inevitability of the feeling at certain times, Hilary immediately has a sense of resentment against Vivian as if he or she were responsible for the jealousy which is felt. Impelled by this resentment, Hilary, under the sway of selfishness, will usually react in one of two ways. Hilary may sulk: pride steps in and Hilary will think: " Why should I allow myself to be hurt by such a person as Vivian? " and the sulking is partly prompted by the hope that it will indicate Hilary's feeling of grievance and partly in the hope that it will result in a particular demonstration of Vivian's affection which, Hilary thinks, will show that Vivian's affection remains unaltered.

More often, perhaps, Hilary will strive to gain reassurance by a different course of action. Hilary will be filled with a restless curiosity; Hilary will cross-question Vivian about the person (real or imagined) who is now regarded as a rival in affection; Hilary will move heaven and earth to find out what seem to be the facts underlying the phenomena which have been the occasion of the outburst of jealousy; Hilary will possibly, in a restless turmoil, spend hours in feverish imaginations of what Vivian may be saying or doing, or, in extreme cases, may even in actual fact follow and watch Vivian and Vivian's actions.

Such sulking and such restlessness on the part of Hilary have two objects: first, to convince Vivian of the fact that Hilary has a real very grievance and, second, to obtain from Vivian some tangible assurance that there is no cause for jealousy and that love has remained unchanged and entire. As we have already seen, such tangible assurances must fail, and Hilary will soon find that the stress of such alternations of elation and despair, the bondage of demands for ever more frequent and convincing displays of Vivian's affection, and the restlessness and suspicion which clouds all lead inevitably to complete frustration.

We need not repeat here what we have already said of the necessity of learning to give and of declaring open war upon the promptings of selfishness. There is but one further consideration which may seem to apply particularly to problems of jealousy. It is a simple one and is merely the logical conclusion of the fact of the uniqueness of the human personality. If each human being be unique, a unique creation of God and unique in God's creation, it must follow that any love or affinity between two persons must itself be unique. In their deepest reality no two human loves can conflict with each other; in the deepest sense there can be no foundation for jealousy.

But we cannot stop here. Human love requires expression, and it is in the realms of love's expression that one love can, or may appear to, conflict with another. A person cannot be with two other persons at the same time, a special gesture of affection is no longer special if it be given to everyone, for those who have given themselves completely to each other in marriage many signs and expressions of affection would constitute a disloyalty to the bonds that have been contracted. Thus, despite the fact that in its deepest reality love can never conflict with love, the expression of one love may easily conflict with the expression of another. We are on difficult ground here, for, while recognizing this fact, we must not imagine (as jealousy would have us do) that all expressions of love for another mean necessarily a conflict with love given to ourselves or that all kinds of love bind in the same way. Thus one friendship, however warm, cannot, save in the jealous imagination, conflict with another. At the opposite end of the scale, the married have the right, and therefore the duty, to demand that the warmer expressions of human love are not bestowed in a manner which could mean a disloyalty to themselves. But even here jealousy should beware of introducing a note of infidelity where none exists; because behaviour may have been injudicious, it does not mean to say that there is a real cause for grievance.

To sum up: on the one hand where love is unexpressed in thought or action the path of one love can never cross that of another; on the other hand, the expression of one love can form a hindrance to another when that expression really implies an infidelity. In all the vast range and varieties of human love it is love itself, the love of Christ, which will be the safe guide not only to behaviour which is right and prudent, but also to behaviour that is kind.

It is little good trying to cure jealousy by logical argument, for jealousy is usually entirely irrational; it is useless to try to cope with it by seeking tangible assurances of affection and loyalty. Jealousy must be overcome by other methods: the ground must first be cleared by a candid acceptance of the possibility of jealousy and thus its presence will not cause dismay or despondency. Then, it must be realized that each time its presence is felt a choice is presented either of loving more or of loving less. The pain will hurt, but love can overcome it and it is love alone that will bring peace. If each pang is resolutely met with by a determination to give more completely and without reserve, in time it will be found that jealousy will trouble little or not at all. Gradually the stage will be passed when love is qualified by the consideration of this or that, and lovers will enter into the peace of love's fruition when the only end of love is itself, its only object God and others, when love has learned by experience that " it is better to give than to receive ".

Again, this may seem to be a hard doctrine, but its rewards are great and frequently are swiftly experienced. A love founded on peace and not dogged by restlessness is a love that will do more than anything else to bring both parties together. The security achieved by the abandonment of a haunting fear of rivalry is love's greatest guardian.

3. POSSESSIVENESS

A sense of insecurity frequently vents itself in possessiveness, the urge to acquire things or persons " for our very own ". Insecurity feels that once it has acquired the sole rights over a thing or a person it has insured itself from danger at all points. The thing or the person is now fenced in, as it were, to form a little private *enclave* safe from all enemies; and, within this *enclave*, its owner imagines that, thus segregated from the rest of the world, the sole use of the thing or the sole attention of the person will be his or hers. Jealousy, also, may lead to possessiveness, but its root cause is insecurity.

Of the manifestations of possessiveness in human love we need say little, for, commonly as they are displayed, there are few subtleties about them. Perhaps the most usual forms are the demand that the whole attention of a person be fixed upon oneself, that the person should have no interests or enthusiasms which are not shared with oneself, that the person should be ready—indeed longing—to be at one's own beck and call, that the person should devote all his or her time and energy to oneself; in short, that oneself should be the total preoccupation of the other person.

These and similar desires will manifest themselves in a variety of ways: Hilary will order Vivian about down to the smallest detail of daily life, Vivian's mind and thoughts must be the reflection of Hilary's, Hilary must be consulted about everything, all other loyalties in Vivian's life must give place to loyalty to Hilary, Vivian must not spend much time with other persons without Hilary's knowledge and approval; Hilary will sum up his or her attitude by telling Vivian that they are all in all to each other, and it does not matter what the rest of the world does. In short, Vivian is rapidly becoming the prisoner of Hilary's " love "; any attempt at rebellion is met by stormy scenes and reproaches, and Vivian is inclined to adopt furtive measures in order to retain at least some small part of independence.

It is a degrading captivity; degrading both for captor and captive. The captor will become ever more masterful and intolerant, even turning the free gifts of love into rights; the captive will in the end either rebel or become the feeble shadow of his or her gaoler. Worn out with exacting demands, tired of endless cross-examinations, longing for freedom, the captive usually rebels, and the captor ponders morosely and cynically upon the fickleness of human behaviour.

Insecurity has sought relief in possessiveness and possessiveness has imperceptibly changed the character of love; the desire to give has turned into the demand to receive and to have. To observe this one has only to study the difference between the state of mind of many engaged couples and their mental outlook some years after marriage: deference has given place to demand, requests to orders, sympathy to impatience; and the whole change marks the collapse of love under the stresses that have assaulted it from within and from without.

Possessiveness strikes at the very heart of love, for love implies the free giving of oneself and, conversely, the acceptance of something freely given. Love is a gift, given and received. The two great commandments of the law, to love God and to love one's neighbour, are not demands which enforce a certain attitude of mind, they are invitations flowing from the fact that God and our neighbour are infinitely worthy of our love and are worthy to be loved, not on account of this or of that, but because of what they are. To put ourselves in tune with love is not to deceive ourselves or to take up some fictitious attitude of mind, but to see things as they are and to follow up that insight with all the power of our wills. But all the time love is a free gift of a free person; it cannot be demanded, may not be forced, is unable to be coerced. Possessiveness, however, tries to demand love as something over which it exercises executive power and imagines that it is in a position to dictate terms to love.

" I will draw all things to myself ", said our Lord, meaning that the insight of his love and lovableness that we get by grace will draw us to him. But our Lord will not force our love, for were he to do so love's very character would be destroyed. When others love us they also are drawn to us by a God-given insight into the lovableness of our unique personality, but, nevertheless, we cannot force love upon them. What they give to us must always be something freely bestowed. To attempt to coerce love or its manifestations is therefore to strike at love's very essence, it is trying to tear the heart out of it—and the metaphor cannot be pressed too hard. And what it attempts must fail, for no power can force what is of its nature free.

What, however, of the case of the married where love has been solemnly promised for ever? Cannot the defrauded husband or wife demand to be loved, demand that vows so solemnly made should be implemented? No, he or she cannot. The married have the right to expect love, if defrauded of it they have suffered a real injury, but they cannot demand what is essentially a free act. We have only got to look at God and the human soul to see an exact parallel: God has created each soul to be loved by him and to love him, he has redeemed it, he has loved it with " an everlasting love "—indeed, so profound is the love that Christ has said, " as the Father has loved me, so have I loved you "—yet, nevertheless, the soul is still " free " to turn away, to reject that love. God has made no demands, has employed no coercion. Disaster and frustration inevitably will follow love's rejection, but, to speak in human terms, God is powerless to force the soul to love him. If God, who is infinite power and infinite love, will not force poor human love, who are we—however wronged and however outraged— to try to employ coercion ?

As we have already said, most possessiveness comes from a sense of insecurity, and therefore the precautions taken by the possessive are usually motivated by imaginary dangers. There are times, of course, when a person has really been " let down " by the waywardness or fickleness of another. Here he may request, may urge, but may never demand love. Indeed, it is useless. As always, the only possible way to obtain the repentance and love of another is to love more and not less, and to continue to love beyond the thought of what might be expected in return. Yet again, we have the paradox that to give is to receive, to lose is to gain; and our task must always be to " launch out into the deep " even if, like the apostles, we sometimes think that we have fished for the whole night and caught nothing. Told to persevere, again they plunged their nets down in the depths beyond sight and sound, and this time they were full.

4. SELF-INDULGENCE

The urge to self-indulgence is perhaps the most direct and obvious manifestation of selfishness in human life;

indeed, few human acts, even the highest, are without their counterpart in self-indulgence. Our most disinterested actions are more often tainted with it than we like to think, our most noble renunciations frequently contain a hidden measure of it and our best resolutions can so easily and so imperceptibly transform themselves into it. Self-indulgence, particularly in love, is ingenious in hiding itself under a variety of disguises: it is quick to put on the garb of common sense, of sweet reasonableness, it is only too ready to plead an inevitability either of character or of circumstances, it is not slow to attire itself in the robes of an angel of enlightenment.

Of its various forms little need be said; not only are they but too familiar, but, at root, they all spring from a single impulse, an impulse which is the exact opposite of love. Love reaches out to someone else for his or for her sake, self-indulgence reaches out to someone else for our own sake. It is as simple as that. Self-indulgence in love means that we are degrading, or attempting to degrade, another person by using him or her as a means of satisfying some pleasurable impulse in ourselves.

It is true that a distinction has here to be made, which is not always an easy one. On the one hand, it is not only impossible not to have pleasure in the love and the expression of the love of another, but it is right and suitable, since the fruition, as opposed to the essence, of love means to love and to be loved. On the other hand, it is self-indulgence and not love to bestow the expression of love *in order* that we may derive pleasure from what in return is bestowed upon us. It is the difficulty of the distinction between a reasonable pleasure in another's love and the giving of love motivated by a desire for pleasure which is often so hard to distinguish either in words or in action.

The clue to guide us here is not so much to be found in any positive rules or standards of behaviour that we can lay down, as in a sober assessment of our intentions in any given situation. We have to ask ourselves: " Is what I am doing, or proposing to do, a valid and fitting sign of love in the circumstances in which I am placed— a real sign of the giving of myself—or is it an attempt to make someone else the mere instrument of my satisfaction ? "

This is a particularly important question where sexual emotion—one of the most powerful of human emotions— is in some way concerned. It is obvious that what is right in some circumstances, for example for engaged couples, is unfitting and wrong in other situations. Circumstances must be our first guide, and an expression of love which goes beyond what is suited to the circumstances is almost sure to be prompted by self-indulgence. The form itself which the expression of love takes is also another guide: there is no need to go into details, but again it is obvious that certain actions are of their nature and in almost all circumstances innocent and right and it is equally obvious that, outside marriage, certain actions can of their nature but be the reflection of self-indulgence. It is true that there is a third category of actions which presents more difficulty, for it consists of actions which *prima facie* and in themselves are not certainly right nor certainly wrong; here we have to go back to the will of God as reflected by the circumstances in which we are placed and to a frank analysis of our motives and our own past experiences if we are to make a valid judgment. On the one hand, we must not be prudish nor narrow, for life should be lived by convictions and not by fears; on the other, we should remember that we are concerned with the most powerful of human passions and the least easily controlled by reason. So much, then, for self-indulgence by way of sexual pleasure.

But there are many other forms of self-indulgence in love, for selfishness has an endless variety of garbs in which it can disguise itself. There is the quarrel engineered in order to enjoy the reconciliation; there is the cultivation of a cloying sentimentality in which all standards of sensibility are sacrificed to a sugary sweetness; there is the deliberate stimulation of the jealousy of another and there is an exclusive preoccupation with another to the neglect of other ties and duties. This may be purely mental and consist in wasting time in romantic day-dreams, so that work becomes scamped and attention to matters in hand only partial, or it may take the form of spending all possible time with the loved one to the detriment of home ties, family arrangements or the just demands of friends; it may mean occupying endless hours writing and re-writing, reading and re-reading, interminable letters and notes. Many of these things are in no way wrong in themselves, but preoccupation with them has been pushed to the point of self-indulgence. Love is being sacrificed to sensation.

The dangers of self-indulgence become even more marked when love has been wounded by one of its other enemies. It is only too easy to try to overcome the pangs of jealousy or the doubts of insufficiency by the apparent antidote of deliberate self-indulgence. The fact that experience shows that self-indulgence provides no answer to love's difficulties can sometimes force people to go even further down that particular road in a kind of desperation, as if they were saying to themselves, " Love has not been real and sure, but this sensation is ". It is, therefore, at the times when difficulties in the path of love seem to be multiplying that self-indulgence is most to be guarded against.

Yet again, it is love and love alone that can provide the answer. In God's love there can be no shadow of self-seeking, it is poured out upon all men beyond thought of return; our love, if it is love, is the love of God and if it is true to itself it must be given to others without consideration of ourselves. It is true that we, weak, fragile and disintegrated as a result of original sin, must love very imperfectly as yet, and self-seeking and self-indulgence must loom large in our lives. This is only to be expected: we should be defying our own experience and sinning against humility if we were at all surprised at ourselves. Nevertheless grace has set us on the right path and with its help love can overcome self-indulgence. The victory will not be without pain, there may be setbacks on the road, but if we continue to will it, the victory is assured. Love overcame the accumulated selfishness of the whole world on the Cross and we share in this conquest every time love overcomes selfishness in us. No great work is completed in a short time and to love perfectly we should have to be saints. Nevertheless, " there is a rest for the people of God ", the peace which comes from love's fulfilment; inasmuch as we may, let us follow the apostle's urging and " hasten into that rest ".

5. FALSE ROMANCE

It is hard to define romance; perhaps the best we can do is to say that romance in its essence is found in an exercise of the imagination by which events or situations are endowed with a content which does not exist in reality. The essence of the romantic attitude is to make a kind of division between things as they are in fact, and the dreamlike and magical quality with which the imagination considers that they should be endowed. We are not thereby condemning all aspects of romance; indeed, a romantic attitude to things is often a salutary relief from the desiccated rationalism of some of its opponents. Unfortunately, however, only too frequently the romantic attitude contains elements of falsehood which must in the end lead to frustration.

It is not the feelings of romance that are at fault; it is surely right and proper to derive a certain satisfaction from an ivy-clad ruin, the murmur of a distant cataract or the lines of a well-loved face. Imagination and feeling have their legitimate notes to add to the gamut of human experience, and to allow oneself to be influenced by certain modern intellectuals who decry all feelings that cannot be brought to the bar of rational analysis, is to deprive oneself of a valuable and creative element in human life. The point where romantic feelings can become dangerous and misleading is reached when they become a substitute for reality, when, under their influence, ordinary things appear to be commonplace and everyday experiences of little significance. No error could be greater: it is the ordinary things of life and the experience of ordinary men that are the usual means of expressing the Christ reigning in human hearts. Because used, touched and experienced by the Christ in us, they become part of that " eternal memory " of which the psalmist speaks. The whole of the sacramental system of Christ's Church is the apotheosis, the transfiguration, of the ordinary: food becomes the body and blood of Christ, water the vehicle by which sin is cleansed in the soul, oil the means by which the consecration of God is given to men. Christianity is not a religion which lives in some vague uplands beyond the ordinary experience of men, it is the transformation of that experience, turning the passing into the permanent, the almost meaningless into the significant, the temporal and local into the internal and infinite. " What God has called holy call not thou common."

If, then, the call of romance results in a despising or a decrying of realities as they are, romance at once becomes false. It imputes false qualities to real things, it tries to escape from present dissatisfactions into a dream world of its own making, it strives for some transcendent experience which, it thinks, ordinary things cannot provide or procure. Dissatisfied with things as they are, romance becomes even more thwarted by them when it compares them with the magical existence of its own creation. In extreme forms it can even despise material things themselves, and it is not without significance that (as indeed the name shows) romance spread into medieval European thought from the Manichees and Cathari of southern France, sectaries who regarded all matter as evil.

Romance, valuable as it is when it leads to a heightening of the sensibilities and to an idealism based upon actual potentialities, can easily become a very great danger to the real growth of love and can lead to difficulties of every possible kind. To begin with, under the influence of romance, a person may not really love another as he or she is; for the romantic, the loved one may easily become little more than a canvas upon which an entirely imaginative and fictitious picture is painted. The loved one is gradually endowed with all possible charms, every profundity of thought, every capability of action; and this process continues until the imagination has constructed a picture of a paragon such as has never been known in this world. True it is that the inmost personality of someone need fear no competition from anyone, but when we turn to someone's qualities—his or her character, behaviour, intelligence or appearance—here we find no such perfection. There is no one without some defect or weakness of mind or character, who does not display some vices, great or small, some inconsistencies of behaviour, some blind-spots in the intelligence, some unexpected pockets of selfishness, some irrational ideas, tiresome habits, self-delusions or any of the other weaknesses to which flesh is heir. To the impartial observer all this is obvious enough, but those who have allowed themselves to indulge in false romance see everything through a mist of delusion. They endow the loved one with every quality, every perfection; nothing that the loved one says or does is wrong, nothing that he or she thinks is foolish.

This transference of the insight of the real value of human personality into an imaginative vision in which his or her qualities are seen as equally unassailable is a most dangerous one. Sooner or later the real truth must come to light: the truth that the loved one shares in the weaknesses of the rest of humanity. To return to Hilary: the romantic Hilary becomes first surprised and then aggrieved; Hilary feels either that Vivian has up to the present been acting a part or that Vivian has deteriorated, probably under the influence of some third party. Hilary considers that Vivian has in some way been entering upon a course of deception by pretending to be other than what he or she really is. Vivian, Hilary thinks, has been acting a part and this is bitterly resented. It never occurs to Hilary that self-deception has been the entire cause of the difficulty and that poor Vivian is completely innocent of any duplicity.

Another form of the self-deception which can spring from romance is perhaps equally, if not more, common. This consists in building up a romantic picture of what love should be. It is natural that under the impetus of love's earlier raptures the lover should imagine that human love provides every possible bliss, insures against every evil and unlocks the door upon an enchanted garden where in perpetual sunshine love can flourish for ever. So much of literature, so much to be seen and heard at the cinema or on the wireless, seems to encourage this vision of other-worldly rapture. Indeed, the words romance and love are now used as if they were synonymous, and love without rapture or glamour would be thought but a pale shadow of what love should be.

And what of the awakening; of the time when dreams have to give place to realities? How often love and romance die together. How often is that first climax of love which we described on an earlier page the very moment when this discovery is made, the moment when, after a growing intimacy, both parties realize that there is nothing more. They have achieved what they sought, they have arrived at their paradise—and it is not another Eden. A kind of sameness seems to descend upon them, the realities of life begin to obtrude themselves, they find that love is not one long transcendent rapture. And how easy is it then to blame the other person, to imagine that love as an ecstatic experience given to others is denied to them because of something withheld, something wanting, in him or her. How great is the temptation again to pursue this imaginative dream, but this time embodied in the person of another. Finally, how common is the spectacle of a tired cynicism which blames the human race for not providing an experience which the romantic thinks ought to have been his and of which he has been defrauded.

Romantic excess is thus a powerful enemy of human love. It leads to day-dreams which at the best are often foolish and wasteful of time, and at the worst can too easily tend to self-indulgence. It can endow the loved one with qualities to which he or she had never laid claim. It can vitiate the very nature of love by imbuing it with a rarefied magic and an imaginative ecstasy which can never long stand the test of real experience. We have used the word " excess " since romance itself is not only inevitable but supplies a deeply felt human need, it is part of the birthright of every emotional love. What we are deprecating is indulgence in romance to the extent of blinding the mind to realities and of making realities seem pedestrian and uninviting. In such an excess is one of the greatest dangers to love to be found, and love should be on its guard against letting imagination assume so commanding a place in its consciousness as certainly to deceive sooner or later.

Love should not be blind. In itself it is the purest and truest insight and, if we have been blinded by it, it is largely through our own fault. We have to learn that it is through things as they are that God works and love grows, that seen in the light of God nothing is ordinary or without significance, and that by the power of God's grace all that is real and true has the potentiality for complete satisfaction and entire fulfilment. In this world we cannot expect to be wholly satisfied; it is a time of shadows and symbols all pointing towards, but not yet fully expressing, the eternal reality. In this life peace has to be fought for, strength is only made perfect through trial, victory is for him who fights. We must not imagine that the path to love's complete happiness can be cleared at a bound or achieved without dust and tears. But, equally, do not let us be discouraged: " I can do all things in him who strengthens me ", and the feelings which accompany the giving of love are bestowed upon us by God to help us along the road, the road that begins in time and ends in eternity. " I shall be satiated when thy glory shall appear ", says the psalmist, and what we now sow in tears we shall reap in an endless ecstasy that surpasses anything that romance can begin to dream, can ever yearn to enjoy.

VI

SOME TESTS OF LOVE

I. UNREQUITED LOVE

PERHAPS one of the most poignant situations in life comes about when someone is yearning to give himself or herself to another who is indifferent to this love or is even irritated by it. The pain of such apparently hopeless love can be one of the most searching experiences of human nature. Having fixed upon some-one whom he or she sees as the only desirable object of love, the lover may undergo every possible kind of torment. The lover may be seared by feelings of jealousy (and no one can help their feelings), racked with a sense of insecurity and tormented by a frustration which it seems impossible that time or circumstances could ever lift.

Every sort of factor seems to combine to increase the anguish of it all. Only too frequently it is the earliest and the most vivid loves of human life, before experience has in some measure tempered the simplicity and urgency of young desire, that tend to be ignored by their recipients. Unrequited love is especially open to the intoxication and the despair of false romance, for there has never been the give and take of actual contact. Thus, those who yearn for love's return are almost bound to view what might have been theirs through golden mists and to idealize the loved one beyond what in fact could ever be. The heart is pining for love, and has convinced itself that the person upon whom it has fixed its gaze is the only one in the world who can provide the satisfaction for which it craves.

Moreover, a frequent cause for such hopeless loving is the faculty which some persons have for falling in love with the idea of love. They long for love and, consciously or unconsciously, they are looking round all the time for someone to fall in love with. Sooner or later they fix upon that someone and he or she becomes the object of their longing; once established as the object, imperceptibly this individual is transfigured in the eyes of the lover and with each transfiguration becomes more an object of desire. Thus a vicious circle is created: the outpouring of love has idealized its object, as its object becomes progressively more desirable love is poured out the more, and this, in turn, feeds the idealization. Quite often the situation is aggravated by the fact that the lover has chosen as the object of his or her longing someone who is, either by circumstances or temperament, entirely incapable of returning the love that is poured out. Almost grotesque situations are therefore created; grotesque, that is, to the external observer, but tragic for the lover.

It is often the custom to laugh at those caught in the toils of such a love, particularly if they are young; but to do so shows a strange absence both of imagination and of sympathy. Anyone who has had to deal with persons so afflicted must long to help them in this time of need. Indeed, cases are not infrequent when persons are so tortured that they can neither eat nor sleep, and it is almost cruel merely to urge such a one to " pull himself (or herself) together " or to make him or her the object of some condescending joke. It is noticeable that the mockery which often seems to greet love's torments comes, not infrequently, from those who have in the past themselves been unhappy and unsuccessful in love and who are now attempting to convince themselves that love is a very humdrum business after all.

Let us say at once that these torments cannot be cured in an hour or a day, but they can to some degree be guarded against. In the first place no one should be surprised to find that his or her love is not returned: particularly with love early in life, for it is hardly to be expected that the first or the second time a heart fixes itself upon someone it will select a person who will return its affection. The odds are heavily against it. It should therefore be remembered that unrequited love is an experience which is at least as likely to occur as not.

Again, there is a moment in love's growth when it is fairly easy to arrest its progress. If a person realizes that he or she is becoming attached to someone, it is at the moment of this realization that it is fairly easy to draw back; not easy, perhaps, but far more easy than it is when love has been freely admitted and encouraged. If the lover can draw back at this point he may save himself much pain in the future; and he (or she) should draw back if the object of love is someone who is already bound by ties that render love impossible or who is manifestly unsuitable for any reason. Thus to offer " love " to the married is to offer degradation. An awareness of the right moment when to call a halt and a resolution in obeying that summons may save months of suffering later on.

Nevertheless, in spite of all we have said, there are many cases of unrequited love where intense suffering is caused through no fault of either party. Nothing but the willing acceptance of pain and the consciousness that the lover is participating in the sufferings of Christ can bring peace. He or she must remember that love cannot, at its deepest level, fail of its object.

There may be no apparent return in this world; yet, deep down underneath human consciousness, provided that the loved one is not in a state of enmity with God, love must essentially be returned: Christ is loving all men in and through each of us, and if Christ lives and loves in the lover and lives and loves in the loved one, both lover and loved must in a very real sense live and love each other and in each other. In this world this may be known by faith alone; in the next, if he " awaits in silence the salvation of God ", the lover will know it by experience and " will be transformed from glory to glory " in it.

There is nothing that can so purify the heart and kill selfishness in us as unrequited love if we go on giving ourselves as the circumstances of the case demand. Events may show us that any open expression of love is impracticable, circumstances may make it clear that such an expression would be wrong, but that should not prevent our loving. The very fact that we cannot give expression to our love, can derive no tangible satisfaction from it, is gradually making it more like the love of God and is refining our hearts so that we are learning how to love those others for whom God is preparing us and them.

It is a hard lesson. But let us remember that with

God nothing is wasted, that each pang of suffering can be, if we make it so, a direct participation in the cosmic battle in which the love of God is conquering sin in us and in the world. Let us remember that God " shall wipe away all tears from our eyes " and that our eyes, no longer blinded by these tears, will see him as he is. They will see that " God is love " and that love is all in all to all.

2. LONELINESS IN LOVE

The fruition of love in this world requires the mutual and unselfish love of two persons. We may give ourselves as best we can to another person, we can crucify selfishness a dozen times a day, we may persevere in patience and affection; but what if the person who has promised to love us and give himself or herself to us ceases to do the same by us ? What if he or she meet our unselfishness with endless demands, our acquiescence with tyranny, our affection with impatience and our expressions of love with scorn ?

It is perhaps even harder to bear the pain of the death of love in another than to endure the sufferings of a love which had never been recognized in the first place. In the former case we have been promised love, we have been told that we are loved, affection has been lavished upon us and we have responded by the giving of our best. We trusted the other person, we believed in him or her and we pinned our hopes upon him or her. We felt secure in this love and we rejoiced in the security which it provided.

Now all has changed. Affection had seemed slowly to decay, an air of indifference had begun to show itself, irritation with us has led to " scenes ", spontaneity and the exchange of ideas and hopes has given way to a gloomy reticence. Doubtless, under the strain, our own patience has sometimes given way; in some stormy scenes we may have " given as good as we got ", we may perhaps have sulked or taken refuge in a pained and pregnant silence or answered with cold and distant civility. Nevertheless, we have on the whole done our best. We have tried to be patient, loving and forgiving, tried to hope for the best and to forget the worst. And now all our efforts seem to have been in vain. " Is it some defect in us ", we wonder, " which has prevented us from retaining the love which was at one time given us ? " The very anxiety of this self-questioning leads us on to a kind of bitterness with the cause of it, and at times we feel like echoing the question of Judas: " Whence is this waste ? "

The loneliness and frustration which come from a lost love cut very deep. Pride, self-reliance, confidence, trust—all are wounded. The future seems dark beyond belief, and we may be tempted to snatch at some satisfaction offered by physical passion in order to still the tumult in our hearts or we may take refuge in the false stoicism of disappointed and wounded pride. If we are not careful we shall certainly become hard and mistrustful and will, with a spurious indifference, smile cynically upon a world which has used us so ill. " Ideals ", we will try to persuade ourselves, " are for the young and untried. I now know life as it is."

" Love believes all things, hopes all things, endures

all things ", and the situation we have to face here differs from that presented by unrequited love. In the first place, if we have solemnly promised our love before God and men in Matrimony we have, like our Lord, " to love our own unto the end ". We may never be able to express our love, our partner may have left us or some calamity like insanity may have afflicted him or her; but our love must still be present. We must not withdraw in spirit. We have promised ourselves and, although circumstances have made the promise impossible to fulfil in action, either wholly or in part, we must not withhold the will to love. This does not mean to say that there are not occasions when we will have to separate physically from our partner; considerations such as the welfare of our children may sometimes demand it or our continued presence in certain circumstances may appear to be a connivance at sin. In the depths of our heart, however, love and not bitterness must prevail.

It is indeed a hard path which we have then to tread; through our misfortune we have been deprived of something which was our right. Nevertheless, we have given ourselves and we cannot go back on what we have solemnly promised and have been given the grace to perform. We have been given the grace to love " for better or for worse " and, though it has been " for worse ", this grace is as powerful in us as ever. In this affliction we are very close to the tears of Christ over Jerusalem, " I would, but thou wouldst not ", and if we are close to his tears we are close to him. We have a companion in our loneliness.

The bonds of love which we have forged outside Matrimony are not so complete. Friendships and engagements have their loyalties but they are not irrevocable in the same way. Even here let us beware of disappointment turning into bitterness and love into hate—for hate and love lie very close to each other. Let us not necessarily imagine that the right always lies exclusively on our side or that we are wholly blameless. If our love had been entirely unselfish it would have done a great deal to have made it easier for our partner to have loved less selfishly; the blame for what has happened may lie in some hidden selfishness in ourselves. In any case we are not in a position to judge, for none of us knows what he or she might do in certain situations or how easily we might fall if certain temptations came before us. Therefore do not let us strike at others in our pain or lose one whit of our belief in love's ideal. We do not know what the future holds and the sufferings of the present prepare us as nothing else can for the loves that may lie ahead.

There is another kind of loneliness in love which we have not yet mentioned, a loneliness which is the fault neither of the lover nor of the loved one but one that springs from the limitations of human nature in this life. This loneliness will be found even in the depths of the most rewarding love and it is a strong, even at times piercing, realization that we have in us abysses which no human intimacy can fill. It is hard to put it into words, but it is an experience of all but the shallowest natures; it is a kind of hunger for fulfilment which nothing can satisfy. At times it may be a vague feeling on the edge of consciousness, at others a positive pain. At root it is a desire for that perfect love and utter understanding which only the love of God can satisfy, a thirst which is the expression of the utmost yearnings of our nature. Almost our Lord's last words before his death were an expression of the thirst of his human heart for love, and it is this thirst that thousands of souls endeavour to slake in internal prayer and which has led them to forsake the solace of much of the expression of human love by becoming a priest, monk or nun: as the older Vulgate version of the psalms says: " My soul has thirsted for God the living spring ".

This thirst and loneliness exists, then, at the root of all human love, but we should not use it as the excuse for trying to drive a wedge between the love of God and the love of man. Real love—the giving of oneself and the suffering which it entails—leads directly to the pure love of God because it is an expression of it. In this life human love can never fully satisfy us because it is the love of Christ within us and therefore its object is infinite and unlimited. We love better than we know. And this love, which is Christ loving in us, can only be satiated with the infinite object of Christ's love—his eternal Father in the depths of the Trinity. With and in Christ we are always stretching out beyond the sacraments of time and place, as the Sexagesima anthem tells us: " Beyond the veil I have cried out, early, early indeed, ' O God, my God, at dawn I wait for thee '." This deep loneliness is tinged with sorrow and yet rich in promise of joy: sorrow, because the day has not yet dawned, and joy, because we know it will.

Let us accept this limitation of human love; still more, let us beware of blaming those whom we love for not supplying what is beyond the power of man to give. It is true that human love is the sacramental expression of that divine love for which the heart aches, but it cannot be a substitute for it. Let us, rather, look upon this loneliness with thanksgiving; it is an earnest that " greater things than these shall you see " and a pledge that all the disconnected fragments of human life will be gathered together in the one love in which God and man alike will share and for which man was made.

3. THE DEATH OF LOVE

Here we are dealing not so much with the pains or the difficulties of love as with love's death, a death that frequently follows upon these pains and difficulties. Love's death may be sudden; love may be killed in some violent explosion or quarrel, may receive a mortal wound in one single deed or even sentence; or love may die almost imperceptibly, interest may slowly abate and affection may gradually wane. But whatever be the character of love's death, its nature is the same. The loved one who, at one time, was the object of a unique interest, of a unique insight, whose every word and action seemed significant and whose affection seemed of infinite worth, has died. Not died physically, but died to us. We are no longer stirred, no longer interested. We wonder what we could have " seen in " him or her, we cannot understand what it was that could have " deceived " us. " Was it the other person ", we wonder, " or was it some strange delusion in ourselves ? " We have a whole stock of reasons to account for what has happened: the other person pretended to be different from what he or she really was, we were young and inexperienced, romance had led us astray by investing the other person with qualities which were not and could not have been present: these and a thousand other considerations pass before our mind. Yet all these reasonings resolve themselves into one word: deception. We have been deceived by another, we have deceived ourselves or we have been deceived in pursuing an ideal of happiness that is non-existent.

But have we been deceived? Very often we have. We may have been in love with the idea of love and have deceived ourselves by focusing that ideal upon a person whom we have never really loved for himself or for herself. We may have allowed ourselves to love someone whom by circumstances or temperament was too removed from us for any real communication between us to have been possible. We may have formed an ideal of a person's character which did not stand up to the stress of reality. We may even in sober fact have been deceived by another person.

Very often, however, we have not been deceived. Our original love was a true insight into the personality of another, our instinct to give ourselves to him or to her was a logical consequence of that insight and the circumstances of both of us made a fruitful and lasting love possible: and yet . . . love has died. What has happened? Is the death of love some inevitable consequence of our condition as limited human beings? When we ask ourselves " what we saw " in someone are we rightly accusing ourselves of self-deception? Have we been pursuing a will-o'-the-wisp and trying to render permanent something which of its nature must be transient? In short, were we being foolish then and are we now wiser than we were?

Such anxious self-questionings can but admit of one answer. Provided that circumstances made our love right and possible from the start, our love was not folly, it was not chasing some impossible ideal, it was one of the most sensible actions of our life. We have been given a great invitation by God to expand the kingdom of his love and, if his will as revealed through circumstances did not forbid our love, its death was a murder for which we are largely responsible.

We had been given a precious insight into the personality of another, we had seen him or her in some measure with the sight of God, we had recognized the infinite lovableness of the human soul and, to begin with, we had co-operated with the grace of God. Then all the enemies of human love arrayed themselves against it and we gave way to selfishness, turned love into self-indulgence, tried to demand tangible assurances of affection or sought a romantic satisfaction that no love in this world could produce. And each time we gave way to any of these temptations we impeded love's growth and sapped its strength. Gradually we changed our attitude from that of loving another for himself or for herself to one of loving another for ourself. Selfishness killed love by degrees and in the end we were left with its decaying corpse. The face which was so full of significance is now almost repellent to us; it is we who have so disfigured it. The words to which we so eagerly listened now merely bore us; it is we who have rendered them void of meaning. The affection we so longed for is now merely tiresome to us; it is we who have destroyed its character.

The death of love gives us a very vivid illustration of

the death of the soul from unrepented mortal sin. By sin the soul has deliberately chosen self in place of God and of God's love; the soul has, as it were, fallen out of love with God, and God, the author of all beauty, life and happiness, seems to it no longer to be significant or an object of desire. If this state persists at the moment of death, the soul—because it does not now see God as a significant object of love—will strive to seek itself as the only good, the only lovable, object of its existence. Thus striving, it will choose that boundless and eternal frustration which we call Hell.

It is not difficult to kill a love, in fact the poet has assured us that all men kill the thing they love, and there are few who have not at one time or another assisted at love's death-bed. Nevertheless, it is not usually an experience which does good either to ourselves or to others. Only too often it leads to a fear of love. Looking back at the experience of a love dead beyond recall, persons will remember all the ecstatic hopes which have proved fruitless, will recollect all the pains of love's dying and will tend, therefore, to be filled with a conscious or subconscious fear of such torments and of such frustrations in the future. They close their hearts to others, they draw back in alarm at any attempted intimacy and they try to persuade themselves that for them love is over. For them, love is pain, is self-indulgence, is disappointment.

And yet how crippled is such a person's power for good. Rectitude unaccompanied by affection is seldom inspiring, sympathy without real human feeling is seldom convincing. It is hard to approach such persons for comfort and help: they are not lacking in goodwill and patience, they are only too anxious to give of their best, but there is something about them which renders all their efforts almost nugatory. They tend to be inhibited, boxed-up in themselves and to raise an invisible barrier between themselves and others. Sometimes they take refuge in a chilling cynicism or, forgetful of the real asceticism that love demands, seek to take a high moral line which condemns all human love as mere weakness and an obstacle on the road to God.

Fortunately nothing is wholly a loss in this life. If the death of love has killed something that might have been of great power for good, yet men can learn much from even so frustrating an experience. They can discover how selfish they really are and have been, they can now understand by experience the great truth that no love can survive of itself without a constant effort to think and to act in terms of giving rather than of receiving, they can now see for themselves that without God all human effort is doomed to frustration.

VII

THE ASCETICISM OF LOVE

"GOD is love and he who remains in love remains in God and God in him"; when we love, as love we must, we have taken the first steps upon a journey that begins in time and ends in eternity, we are starting to learn how to express the love of God in human experience and how to include in that love as many as possible of those around us. In the order of experience we cannot love everyone; we cannot express love for those who are separated from us by distance, for we have never seen them; or by time, for they were born before us or will be born after us; or by circumstances such as must make our contact with them superficial and transient. There are, however, some persons who are chosen by God especially for us and we have been chosen for them, and it is these whom in various ways we can love in the order of experience. Each love will be different, will differ with the person, with our relationship to that person, with our status in regard to that person, but each will be a real reflection of the love of God within us. Emotion may be present or absent, but love lies deeper than feeling.

Do not let us, therefore, be afraid of love. Love can never sin, "seeketh not its own", cannot stand between the soul and God. Nevertheless there are some writers who, either directly or by implication, give the impression that human love must imply some kind of self-indulgence, must in some way be opposed to the " pure " love of God. It is perhaps natural that this should appear so at first sight: love is apparently so often the road to self-indulgence, the cause of jealousy and selfish pre-occupation. But here appearances are misleading: on the psychological level love is not the cause of jealousy or of self-indulgence but its revelation. The lover lives on a plane of an altogether heightened sensibility, he is beginning to discover himself as he really is, and part of that discovery must be that of the selfishness and self-indulgence of fallen nature. At a deeper level, too, it is obvious that selfishness must become more apparent for, seeing its inner citadel invaded, it exerts all its power to thwart the progress of love.

Love cannot, then, cause selfishness, jealousy or self-indulgence, it can only bring out into the open what was already latent. Those who lay such emphasis upon the dangers of human love and upon the prudence of remaining aloof have little that is constructive to offer. Virtue must overcome vice, not retreat ignominiously before it; charity cannot exist in a vacuum apart from any expression of it in human experience, while purity is a positive quality of love and not the mere negation of lust. The love of man, provided it is love, cannot conflict with the love of God, for love cannot war against itself. Nor, moreover, can this retreat from selfishness be considered to be a means of carrying out the apostle's ideal for the Christian, " mortified according to the flesh, made alive in the spirit ". The abandonment of love may be a heavy mortification, and indeed be a mortification that some circumstances demand, but it can never be a mortification so searching as that required for the growth of love. Experience shows that real love is a consuming fire which burns in its purgatorial flames all the promptings of selfishness. " Thou hast tried me in the fire and no sin in me is found "—these words of the psalmist show us where true mortification lies and what is its reward.

We cannot do better than follow the programme of mortification laid down by St. Paul in his first Epistle to the Corinthians, and if we take it clause by clause we shall see that it embodies the whole of that crucifixion of selfishness which is essential to love's maturity and happiness and in which alone can we be made secure in love.

" Love ", says St. Paul, " is patient."[1] Love, there-fore, can afford to wait, is not in a hurry for reciprocation, can bear with the defects of others, is patient with its own defects. To build the edifice of love is a long and mighty task, and love knows how to wait, to refrain from forcing on a situation with impetuous haste, knows that even the greatest difficulties can be overcome if God so will.

Yet really to be patient in love is to be greatly mortified: there is a natural urge for quick results and easy satis-factions, there are many times when those whom we love must try our patience almost beyond belief (for it is a fact of human experience that it is for the most part only those whom we love who can really annoy us), there are times when we will ask ourselves " how is all this going to end? " forgetting that love does not wish to " know

---

[1] We have used the late Mgr. Knox's translation here, save that we have rendered " chaitry " as " love " for the sake of greater clearness.

the times and the moments which the Father has put into his own power ".

" Love is kind." Kindness is the courtesy which springs from true love, it is the particular quality of unselfishness in action. To be kind means not only to be patient, but to treat another with respect and reverence, not to be exacting or imperious. Again, how hard it is always to be kind to those whom we love: the demands of passion may result in positive unkindness, possessiveness certainly leads to it and self-indulgence nearly always results in it. To be kind always and on every occasion is an asceticism which, though it does not display itself in some tremendous act of renunciation, demands constant self-control and thought of others.

" Love feels no envy." Jealousy and envy are, as we know, perhaps the strongest and commonest enemies of love. The occasions of them are so numberless and our sense of insecurity is so great that self-love is always tending to fasten upon them. It is certainly no easy thing to crush down the pangs of jealousy, especially as they have a way of recurring again and again. The pangs, of course, we cannot help feeling, but generously to turn them into an invitation to love more deeply and to trust more completely is a searching mortification. That the emotion of jealousy has, as a rule, little or no counterpart in reason makes the task more difficult, for our intellect is here largely powerless. We can thus seldom overcome jealousy by the—perfectly true— considerations of our reason; we have to mortify selfishness at a deeper level by learning how to give beyond thought of what we may or may not receive in return. Here, surely, is one of the greatest asceticisms of love.

" Love is never perverse or proud, never insolent."
Pride, perversity and insolence are all very close to each
other, for perversity is frequently the expression of pride
in action and insolence its expression in words. Love,
more than anything else, is an onslaught upon pride and
self-sufficiency. Pride does not like having to admit that
it needs another person for its happiness, and frequently
self-love will try to say, " X is not necessary for my
happiness, I need no one. I can stand upon my own
feet." There are moments in all human love when this
sense of dependence becomes an affront to pride, and
only too often wounded pride will become perverse in
action by deliberately doing the opposite of what it
thinks the loved one will expect it to do. It may express
itself by a determination to be frigid in manner when
the loved one is expecting a display of affection, or it
may, perhaps, show itself coldly disposed towards plans
which the loved one projected in order to give pleasure.
Perversity will strive to appear calm and aloof when
another is agitated, to appear bored when another is
interested, to be lazy when another feels energetic.
Insolence is that perversity's expression in words.

Humility, in the form of an admission of dependence
upon another, comes with difficulty to us. Our Lord
condescended to human weakness by feeling the need
for companionship in his Agony at Gethsemane, but we
like to imagine that we have no such weakness, that no
one can give us anything that we have not got already.
The admission in thought and action that others are
necessary for us, that we are incomplete and insufficient
without them, is an admission as necessary for the
growth of love as it is hard to human pride. In the

crucible of love pride is mortified and humility comes into its own. But pride cannot perish without pain: it is love that makes the pain bearable, the suffering fruitful.

" Love does not claim its rights." To claim its rights is the first instinct of human insecurity, for insecurity feels somehow that the recognition of its rights by others will give that status in the eyes of the world and that importance in its own eyes which it so much desires. As we have seen, this attempt to overcome our sense of insecurity by the artifices of self-esteem, and in particular by laying an extravagant emphasis upon what we think is due to us, is bound to fail. We can only really be rooted in what is true, in what is eternal. Moreover, insistence upon our own rights is completely opposed to that giving of ourselves which is the essence of love.

Nevertheless, our " rights " tend somehow to become almost sacred in our eyes, we are almost tempted to believe that any infringement of them is an infringement of the divinely ordained ordering of human society. In love, particularly, selfishness is always urging our rights upon us and telling us that their implementation by the loved one is a sure sign of his or of her love. We have rights it is true, but love should look beyond them in its movement from ourselves to another, should abandon all rights—save for those which are bound up with our duty to God and to others—in the costly renunciation to which it invites. Insufficiency must kick away the scaffolding which has so long and so uneasily propped it up and we have to lose all to find all, to exchange the shadow for the substance.

" Love is not provoked." The disappointments and difficulties which attend human love can so easily display themselves in irritation with the loved one, an irritation which may express itself in stormy scenes, recriminations and outbursts of anger. The anger of those who love is strange and rather terrible: it acquires an added bitterness from the fact that the lover knows that he or she should not be angry and even more from the fact that love's anger is almost a kind of masochism. Hurting the loved one, the lover is hurting himself at the same time and the thrusts impelled by anger usually strike deeply at vulnerable points. The very irritation with itself which such anger fosters exacerbates further the furious frustration which it expresses.

It is peculiarly difficult not to be provoked by someone one loves: selfishness, jealousy and pride sometimes seem to array themselves together in a common onslaught which focuses itself upon the loved one who has become the symbol of all this frustration. To mortify the desire to " have it out ", to check the urge for a " full explanation ", to refrain from " making the position clear "— all these can cut very deep. Love, however, must know how to *laisser tomber*, know when not to probe too deep, must refrain from angry recrimination or irritated self-justification. To love completely means not only to give, but to forgive.

" Love does not brood over an injury." This is really the logical consequence of the abandonment of our " rights ". Many of the injuries that love receives do not really exist at all, they have been conjured up by our imagination to rationalize our feelings of doubt and jealousy. Foolish as it is to manufacture such " injuries ", it is much more foolish to brood morosely over these idiot children whom we have conceived and whom we

are now nursing. Sometimes, of course, we have really
been injured; we have been treated with disloyalty or
our trust has been betrayed; here again, quite apart
from the futility of brooding upon an injury (which is
perhaps one of the most unconstructive of human
actions), love will look beyond to reality. We have
loved and the object of our love is a human person who
by nature and grace is infinitely lovable. Our love was,
therefore, neither foolish nor blind. Nevertheless, the
fact that we have suffered some real injury does not
impair the rightness of our original dedication, for it is
not the person who has changed, it is merely his or her
actions, his or her modes of thought. Personality
remains unimpaired no matter how grievously action
may traduce it or temperament betray it. Injury is,
then, no excuse for ceasing to love. There are occasions
when we may have to cease from the expression of love,
but love itself should never die, just as the love of God
has never died for the greatest and most deliberate sinner
upon the earth.

To refrain from brooding over an injury may range
from the simple renunciation involved in forgiving a
hasty word to the preservation of an undaunted affection
for someone for whom in the future we may never be
able to express our love and for whom our love is of no
value. It may, therefore, be merely a slight mortification
or it may be an asceticism which sifts the very soul.
Whatever it is, love will embrace it and love will provide
the strength to sustain it. It was Love itself which
taught us to say: " Forgive us our trespasses as we
forgive them that trespass against us ".

" Love takes no pleasure in wrong-doing." Here we

are dealing quite simply with the threat to love posited by self-indulgence, for self-indulgence is always urging an immediate satisfaction at love's expense. In particular is this the case where illicit sexual pleasure is concerned: under the plea for warmer affection sexual passion is frequently impatient to indulge itself. The age-old pleas of the seducer, " If you really loved me . . .", " But we love each other . . .", show how wrong-doing can be urged under the name of love. Yet all sin is of its nature utterly opposed to love: sin offers moral or material degradation, love offers salvation; sin profanes, love reverences; sin unites in a bond of self-seeking, love in a bond of selflessness. That the bond of love should be turned into a compact to commit sin of whatever kind is an utter denial of the nature of love, is almost inevitably to deal it a mortal wound.

In spite of all this, it is true that both circumstances and temperament may make the refusal to turn love into an occasion of wrong-doing a very deep mortification. Those who are engaged for long periods with no hope of marriage in the near future have much to endure, those whose temperaments have endowed them with quick sensibilities or strong passions may find that love provides them with the opportunity for real asceticism. Finally, the consciousness that underneath all the apparent frustrations of their situation love must be growing in strength is not one that comes easily. Often it is discovered only after a long period of time and much suffering. Love's war with self-indulgence may be a hard-fought and bitter one, but in the end love will have its victory when the truth of the apostle's words will be realized that " the things which we see are the things of time, but the things which we do not see are the things of eternity ". Love must yearn for the eternal or it is not love.

" Love rejoices in the victory of the truth." To love is to give oneself to what is. It is part of the essence of love that the gift of oneself which it evokes is a gift which is of infinite worth made to one who is of infinite worth. Love is therefore truth in action. False romanticism can cloud this action of truth and doubts can assail it, but in essence love and truth are one.

Love cannot, therefore, flourish in an atmosphere of dishonesty or pretence, lies cannot really further its growth however much they may seem to for a short time. Love offers true selfhood to another and knows that, though this offering is " for better or for worse ", the " better and worse " apply only to what is not of the substance of love (circumstances, defects of temperament, all that is part of a man and his actions outside the personality itself) and the offering is made at the altar of truth. It is so hard, however, for poor human nature, beset as it is by doubts and lack of confidence, to make the gesture of complete trust which the abandonment of all that is not absolutely real in it entails. Human nature longing, reasonably enough, to paint itself in its best colours so often employs a false dye, or tends to adopt a pose, to overlook a difficulty or to try to blind others to its defects. Honesty, the positive expression of truth, appears to introduce an element of risk and it is often so much easier to say nothing or to speak the word that soothes. Love alone will help us to distinguish occasions when tact and kindness demand our silence from those when not to speak is an act of cowardice and tantamount to perpetuating a lie. Love alone can give that real conviction which, hard as it is to human nature, will not hesitate to dissipate falsehood and will enable it to have the strength to appear and to be what it is. The mortification of the human instinct always to take the easier and pleasanter course is one which is necessary for love's growth. If this asceticism be pursued, experience will soon show that with love, as with everything else, truth is not merely a matter of duty but an occasion for rejoicing. It is the key to that happiness which he alone can give who said: " I am the truth ".

" Love sustains, believes, hopes and endures to the last." Why can love sustain and endure to the last? It is the consequence of its belief and the hope following upon that belief. For love to " believe to the last " does not imply any kind of credulity or wishful-thinking about the character or temperament of the loved one or about the nature of love's experience; it is the recognition by the mind and heart that another is in himself or herself worthy of our love and it is a belief in the worthiness of love itself. If " the saints by faith have conquered kingdoms " what must not be the victories in store for love? Love sees the measureless possibilities for good in another, love looks beyond the present to eternity, sees the real personality through the defects of fallen nature. Love possesses the vision of the truth and is possessed by it. It knows that " all shall be well ", that all is well save sin alone. Therefore, in " hoping to the last " it is not indulging in the wishful-thinking of romance but is basing its hope upon the true vision which it has been given. Its belief and its hope are boundless. It will sustain all anxieties, endure all calamities, overcome all doubts and survive all disasters. Belief will penetrate deeper than sense and hope will soar above appearance. Faced with destruction, love, undismayed, awaits a new creation; obscured by the darkness of shadows and symbols, love, undeterred, rejoices in the possession of reality. Wearied but unflagging, bruised but never broken, defeated in one battle after the other but certain of ultimate victory, love endures beyond place, beyond time and beyond death. Sustaining all things, believing all things and hoping all things, it stretches out through the crucifixion of sin and selfishness to the transformation and fulfilment of the resurrection. Sure of its ultimate and eternal triumph, it awaits in complete confidence that end which the psalmist terms " the end of all ending ".

VIII

THE TRIUMPH OF LOVE

WE have dwelt long upon the difficulties that lie in love's path and the searching asceticism which love demands; our purpose has been in part to show that many of the troubles that beset human love come from a lack of awareness of the obstacles which love must overcome and in part to demonstrate our contention that the continuance of love requires a far higher degree of mortification than love's negation. It has not, however, been our intention to paint the difficulties with such vividness as to make it appear that love requires so high a degree of unselfishness that to love properly is almost impossible for those not far advanced in sanctity. It is true that love does demand a very high degree of unselfishness, but it is equally true that love has allies so powerful that there should be no need for fear.

First of all, on the purely natural level, there is an attraction for the other person, a reaching out towards him or her, a satisfaction in loving and being loved, which not only responds to one of the deepest urges of human nature but ranges human feeling powerfully upon the side of love. Thus, when love and affection are present and felt, it is easy to take the first steps towards self-renunciation, the instinct to give is a far deeper and more real one than the instinct to grasp and natural affection is powerful to draw it out of the hidden recesses of the human spirit. At least in the first stages emotion can be a powerful aid to love, and under its influence much that is hard or difficult can be made easy. As a writer has recently said, " When we make the distinction between nature and grace, we must not forget that nature is in itself a grace ". The whole of human nature has not been vitiated by the sin of Adam and, although selfishness is always with us, our nature itself at its deepest level is on the side of love.

If this be so in our natural life, how much more is this the case with the new life that is given to us by grace. Among our assets—if so we may term them— we have not only our dignity as adopted children of God but all that prayer and the sacraments can give us to enable us to be in action what we are by grace. We have the whole Church fighting for us on our side— those praying for us on earth, those suffering in love's flame in purgatory and those who, now in glory, are ever striving to make us share more deeply in the triumphant love that is theirs. We do not have to enter the battle without weapons.

By Baptism we are plunged into the very state of love, for by it we receive the life of Christ into our souls. We live in him and he lives in us. We act through him and he acts through us. The love which he pours out upon his Eternal Father and with which the Father loves him is the Holy Ghost, the Spirit of Love: and into that love Baptism has plunged us. Far beyond sight, sound and feeling the love of God springs up from the depths of our hearts. Our Baptism was the work of a moment, its waters washed our heads for a brief second, but deep within us its tides are for ever flowing. Deep within us that living water is springing up in our hearts in fulfilment of our Lord's promise to the baptized: " From his heart living waters shall flow ".

The Apocalypse tells us that this water is " the water of life given to us freely ". In the world of nature water cleanses all impurities, gives life to the growing plant and quenches thirst: always and at all times it is striving to reach the sea where alone it can find its level, where alone it can come to rest. So is it with this water of life of which our hearts are the perennial spring: our impurities are washed away by it, the seed of eternal life draws nourishment from it—as the psalmist tells us, " in its dewfalls the growing seed shall rejoice ", our thirst for unending love and life is quenched by it and always and for ever, night and day, recognized or un-recognized, it is moving on to that great sea of peace and rest which St. Catherine of Siena calls " the sea pacific of the divinity ".

By Baptism, then, our hearts become springs of life, " fountains of water springing up to eternal life ", as we read in St. John, and, if springs of life, then fountains also of love, for the life of God is the life of utter and measureless love. By Baptism we have it in us to love, the power and force of eternal love is given to us. We have not to depend upon the transient impulse of some resolution, the precarious pursuit of some ideal or the doubtful attainment of some happiness which we cannot believe will be ours. At root we already possess the love for which we long; Baptism plants it in us in a growing state and, unless we deliberately cripple that growth, it must attain to leaf and flower and fruit.

In this world love cannot come to fruition without pain: the baptized can face this suffering with confidence, for Baptism has not only planted the seed, it has given all that will enable the seed to grow. We suffer, it is true, but, being one with Christ, in a very real sense our sufferings are his and his ours. We are not, therefore, suffering alone: Christ is with us and in us. We are not, therefore, suffering in vain for we are participating in those sufferings of Christ which led directly to his resurrection and victory. All our suffering is valuable and creative: it is the means through which love overcomes the obstacles placed in its path. No moment of it is wasted, nothing is being lost: for every pang we endure in Christ is making us more perfect agents of love and making our love more pure, more valuable and a better gift to another.

If we analyse our feelings we can easily see the difference between unhappiness and suffering. Unhappiness, which has always its roots in thwarted selfishness or self-indulgence, produces a kind of flatness, a sense of frustration which can quickly lead almost to despair. Unhappiness tends to revenge itself by attacking others or abusing the circumstances which it thinks have caused it. It is destructive, impotent and impoverishing. Suffering, however, is altogether different. The circumstances or the person which have caused it may be identical with those which produced unhappiness, but the response is quite otherwise. Suffering, the pain of crucified love, may bring with it pangs that seem almost too great to be borne. Almost, but not quite, for God's love in us is always stronger than our human weakness. The pains of suffering are, nevertheless, creative, invigorating and constructive. Through them love is purified and gains in strength, belief does not turn to mistrust nor hope to despair. Happiness, moreover, is not lost but persists in and through the deepest suffering. It is then that the soul becomes aware, almost by experience, that " the sufferings of this present time work for us a far more exceeding and eternal weight of glory ".

It is Baptism that enables the soul to remain undismayed by the prospect of such suffering, that gives it strength to pass through it undeterred, that gives to human suffering a redemptive character. " Do not fear, if thou dost pass through the midst of the fire I shall be with thee ", says the Church on the feast of St. Laurence and, indeed, fear is not for us. Love may have to pass through pain, but unhappiness need never be its lot; it may have to learn to wait, but success is inevitable and sure; it may have to abandon a particular form of union with a particular person, but a closer and more ecstatic union with everyone for ever is promised in the future. Christ has gone before us: the totality of love has met and has overcome the utmost pangs of human suffering. He has shown us the way. But he has not merely pointed out the way to us, he is the way; living with him and loving with his love we too " must pass from death to life because (we) have loved the brethren ". With him and in him we need neither fear the future nor doubt the present: " I can do all things in him who strengthens me ".

Confirmation is especially a sacrament of love, for by it the Holy Ghost, the Spirit of love, comes into our hearts in order to help us to translate that love which

Baptism gave us into action. By Confirmation we are
enabled, and in a measure consecrated, to become active
in the spread of God's kingdom, a kingdom of love;
able, as soldiers of Christ, to bear the wounds which love
inflicts on selfishness. Confirmation is thus particularly
the sacrament that will give us that fortitude which the
growth of love demands.

There are two ways in which this fortitude is especially
necessary for the lover. In the first place, shyness,
diffidence and timidity have very often to be overcome.
How often are those who love afraid to express what
they feel, hesitating perhaps on account of the difficulty
of finding words or wondering anxiously how their
declaration will be received. How often do lovers make
a resolution to speak openly, they may even select
mentally a particular time or place for their revelation,
and then, when the moment comes or the place is reached,
confidence fails them and, the declaration unmade, they
reproach themselves for lack of courage.

A far higher degree of courage is required to withstand
all the difficulties that will make themselves felt during
the course of love: to remain resolute despite a lack of
response, to endure the sufferings caused by real defects
in the loved one, to overcome all the threats to love
which our own selfishness may conjure up—all this
requires a very high degree of courage. And this
courage is given by Confirmation in which the soul
directly participates in the dynamic action of God's grace.

Our Lord compared his Spirit to the wind, and the
first coming of the Holy Ghost to the Church was marked
by the sound of a great gale. "The wind", our Lord
tells us, "bloweth where it listeth and you hear the

sound thereof, but no man knoweth whence it cometh nor whither it goeth, so is everyone that is born of the Spirit." The wind is always in movement, always urged along to distant horizons. Coming from the great spaces of the skies, it breathes life into stagnant water, blows away fogs and mists, replaces the fetid staleness of the dead air of the back streets with refreshing and renewing sweetness, cools the sultriness of still heat and makes the seemingly dead trees and grass spring into a life which moves with its gusts. Invisibly it wraps itself round everything upon the earth. So it is with the Spirit of love. To merely human consideration its movements are unpredictable, its actions seemingly capricious. Why who loves whom is a question that can seldom be answered completely, for it is part of the providence of God which alone knows what is best for each. The Spirit, like the wind, brings movement and life into what is stagnant and still: our hearts which may so easily become cold and sterile are stirred into activity by God's love as the angel stirred the dead waters of Siloam. The Spirit of God breathes the spaciousness of God's infinity into our cramped notions, our petty ideals and our cheap satisfactions. It blows away the mists and fogs of false romance, breaks up the clouds of jealousy and cools the fever of passion. Unseen and known only by the life which it brings, the Spirit of God permeates creation and wraps all round with its presence. And that Spirit is love, which, with all its strength and might and pervasiveness, we receive at Confirmation.

Our Lord also called his Spirit the Paraclete, or Comforter, and our reception of it at Confirmation means that we gain not only in love itself and in the strength of that love, but we receive also love's consolation. The Spirit does not necessarily console by any alleviation of pain, it does not provide any easy way of escaping suffering or pet us with some facile consolation: it reaches deeper than feeling, further than thought. The comfort given by the Spirit is a deep peace which exists beyond and through all the tears which, as the old poet said, lie at the heart of things. The peace of God which passes all understanding is one founded upon a profound sense that love is the ultimate reality and that love is at this moment triumphing if we will only let it do so. This peace looks beyond the moment to the eternal, it is conscious that while love's pain is but for a time love's victory is for ever. Confirmation enables us to be happy in the midst of suffering and at peace in the midst of pain; it makes us able to understand and almost to feel the truth of those profound words of Julian of Norwich: " It is better that a man should be taken from pain than that pain should be taken from man."

The Eucharist is the food of love, for love is offered and love is received. At Mass we offer to God, under the form of bread and wine, everything that we have and are, and our love cannot be absent from this offering. Whether we are filled with satisfaction in love, whether our love has been unrequited, whether we are trying to cope with the difficulties of love or whether we seem to be crushed under love's burdens, whatever be our situation we offer up our love for what it is and as it is. Christ, being one with us, must identify himself with our offering; he offered himself in love to his Father on the cross and he offers himself still in everlasting glory at the Father's right-hand; thus it is that our offering of ourselves becomes his offering, himself, and the offering of our love becomes the offering of his love.

We have given and in the Eucharist we receive. We have made, under the poor symbols of human food, the offering of ourselves and of our feeble and halting love; in return we receive Christ, we receive eternal love, "the fullness of the Godhead corporeally". By his love our love is nourished, by his offering our offering is made significant, by receiving him we receive all that the heart of man can desire, the possession of that love for which we long.

By the Eucharist, then, love is fed, for the Eucharist is the memorial of Christ's love, his last gift to us before his Passion. It was this love of Christ which led him through suffering to resurrection, and that love is given to us to lead us through pain to glory. This reception of victorious love is not only the pledge that love will triumph in us, but the very means by which it can do so. Bodily food fills the hungry, revives the weak and strengthens the weary: this divine food satisfies that hunger for love which exists in every human heart, revives us in moments when we feel that all is over and "we can no more", strengthens us when we are weary of well-doing and life seems to stretch out before and behind us in an endless procession of broken resolutions. It is upon the Eucharist that we can build our strength, our courage and our hope, for not only does it feed love, it is love. "Can you drink the chalice which I am about to drink?" Fed by the Eucharist and not trusting to our own strength, we dare to answer, "We can".

By Penance love's wounds are healed. We are for ever failing in love. We fail by omission: we are indifferent or cold, heedless, lazy, self-preoccupied, unable to bother, take no pains to do our best for another, cultivate a "splendid isolation", display our boredom, remain unresponsive and inert and are quick to disguise our dislike of being involved with another's happiness by invoking excellent maxims about "minding our own business". We also fail positively: we are selfish, possessive, jealous, self-indulgent, unreasonable, quarrelsome, disloyal, mendacious and insincere—indeed, every sin will be found in essence to be denial of the love of God or of man.

We are, then, always inflicting wounds upon love. Some are calculated, some almost beyond our willing, some are trivial and some are deadly. This is, perhaps, an unwelcome truth, but any examination of our own behaviour over a period of time will at first tend to depress us by the record of its constant lapses from the ideals for which we have striven. It is here that Penance comes in. If we confess our faults and make our resolves to do better, we are freeing our minds from their heavy burden. At any time we can make a fresh start, unhampered by the consciousness of past failure, and in applying the salve of absolution to our self-inflicted wounds we are putting ourselves into a position to cope with what lies ahead, for we have by hard experience gained a more real and genuine outlook upon love and its problems. We have begun to understand that the fruits of love cannot be grasped immediately or its perfection attained in one impulsive leap. We have learned more about ourselves and our weaknesses and we have faced up to them fairly and squarely.

In Penance, we have admitted our faults and have asked God to blot them out; it is easier, therefore, for us to resist that temptation which comes to all at some time or another, the urge, namely, to resurrect the past failings of others and to confront them with them. Few things can so hinder the course of love as this habit of carrying over a grievance from day to day, few things are more injurious than to amass an armoury of past grievances to be employed as offensive weapons when we feel irritated with another. " Let the dead bury the dead ", said our Lord, and, if we refuse to let the un-pleasantness of the past fade into oblivion, we must inevitably lay ourselves open not only to a retaliation in kind but to a poisoning of the very wells of love. Nothing is so destructive of peace, especially in a family, as the revival of forgotten injuries, and the grace of Penance will enable us to let the failures of others rest in that oblivion into which our own have been consigned. The frank admission and the full forgiveness of our own infractions of love will give us new heart to face the future unafraid. Unfettered by the past, we can face the present and the future with added confidence; we must not, therefore, try to bind others with the chains which, by God's grace, we have cast off from ourselves.

One of the effects of the sacrament of Extreme Unction is to prepare us for death, not only by the forgiveness of our sins, but also by an effective grace which will enable

us to face death as we should.   Death is to purely human
eyes the extinction of love.   Life, movement, thought,
even consciousness of selfhood, appear to go and it seems
as if love has received its final and lasting defeat.
Paradoxically, however, death is love's most triumphant
hour, for the moment of death is the moment when love
is forced to exist in its own right; unsupported by
human consolation, inexpressible in human contacts,
love must now renounce all that is not itself.   Love
cannot die, even though every form of its expression and
every sign of its presence must share in the death which
sin has brought upon the human race.   Love cannot die
because it is part of that risen life of Christ in the soul
which has already overcome sin and death; if death
" has no longer any dominion " over Christ, it can no
longer have any dominion over his love which must live
on beyond time, circumstance and appearance.

Yet, if death leads directly to love's triumph, it is a
triumph that must be preceded by the most complete of
all renunciations.   At death we have to renounce all
visible evidence of love's continuance, every means of its
expression.   If it is we ourselves who die, we are making
the supreme sacrifice, the final offering of ourselves into
the hands of God, renouncing completely every tangible
assurance, every human safeguard, everything that is not
ourselves.   It is the hour of pure faith, unhesitating
trust and that complete love which comes with complete
giving.   If it is others who are dying, we have to renounce
all tangible evidence of their continued existence, every
sign and expression of love, everything that is not themselves.   In either case the renunciation is a hard and
searching one.   In our own case it means a complete

trust in what to the senses is unknown, in what is so alien to the determination of our fallen nature to judge by visible and tangible evidence that all is well. In the case of others it implies an entire belief and trust that love and existence will prevail unimpaired after every visible sign of their presence has passed away.

Extreme Unction enables love to face this solemn moment without hesitation, if not without pain. Its grace enables us who receive it to go forward into eternity with the sure knowledge that we are taking love with us, that we are to be joined more closely to those we love than before was possible, that signs and expressions of love are now fading away into the complete reality which they have embodied so ineffectively, that what words could not fully reveal is now to be imparted in deed, that our visible presence which, perhaps, conceals rather than reveals what we are, is to be exchanged for the hidden presence of ourselves in full reality. And when those whom we love die, it is open to us to share in the grace of the sacrament they have received by knowing that what is being wrought in them is the greatest possible pledge for our everlasting union in the future. We would not be human did we not grieve, but in and beyond our sorrow prevails the deep sense that " your sorrow shall be turned into joy, a joy which no man shall take away from you ".

Holy Order and Matrimony are twin sacraments of love and should be considered together, for both are directly concerned with the spread of God's kingdom of love. By Holy Order a man is raised by grace to a state in which he can impart the sacraments he is ordained to give and he is enabled to carry out all that his office as mediator between God and man may entail. To be ordained is to be a priest of love: not only by imparting love as minister of most of the sacraments of the Church, but by ministering love to all men. The love of the priest is that higher kind of love which remembers our Lord's words, " It is better to give than to receive "; it is a love that should give itself to all without consideration of return. The very promise of chastity which the priest makes shows that he renounces, not love, but the full human expression of reciprocated human love; not that that expression is wrong or is something reluctantly permitted to men, but it is an expression which of its nature implies receiving as well as giving. The priest, like our Lord himself and like his Mother, gives himself in love to all with no consideration or even hope of return.

It is no inhuman, remote, cold love that the priest must give: he must really love, really care about people. But he must really love and care not for himself but for themselves. On the one hand, he must not, by a simulated interest and a feigned affection which is never translated into human feeling, use other people as mere instruments of his own private spiritual perfection, for he must love them and not himself; on the other hand, he must be always on his guard against favouritism and intimacies of a kind that could lead to self-indulgence or selfish preoccupation.

The greatest safeguard of a priest's love (and the same, of course, also applies to monks and nuns) is his promise of chastity. Chastity is not the denial of love; indeed, it would hardly be too strong to say that a promise of chastity is a promise of love. It is both a promise to love God above all created things and it is a promise to love others without thought of response. For those who are called by God to make it, it is a special invitation to a special relationship with him and a special relationship with his creation; a relationship which directly reflects God's own love for men. By his promise of chastity the priest must love the responsive as well as the unresponsive, the tiresome as well as the pleasant, the interesting as well as the dull. He must love when he feels like it and when he does not feel like it. He must despair of no one, however abandoned; he must forgive all injuries, however unprovoked; he must interest himself in all details, however trivial; he must believe in the existence of and must search for the treasure hidden in the most unpromising field.

All this is hard for fallen nature which longs to call a halt to this perpetual giving of love, longs to rest awhile in some relationship where love is received as well as given. Certainly, if love be given it will be received—indeed, in a manner passing all expectation—but each such reception must be a call to further giving. The priest may not rest; helped on his way by such consolations as God has given him and taught by humility not to despise them, he must go on further and give more. He must give all to gain all. In the strength of the sacrament he has received and which is renewing itself from day to day in him, he can face this long pilgrimage of love unafraid.

By the sacrament of Matrimony the complete mutual giving of man and woman in love is sanctified and by it the love given and received is made an effective expression

of God's love. To live the life of chastity with its
constant demands upon love and its renunciation of so
much that the human expression of love can give is not
an easy thing; equally, the life of the married makes
great demands upon the reality of love. Married life
has its own very real difficulties: it is not easy for two
differing temperaments always to run in harmony, there
are aspects of the character of either party that will
remain forever baffling to the other, either party will
have much to forgive the other. The presence of children
brings other difficulties in its train: financial stress, the
wear and tear of looking after them, their apparent
unresponsiveness on occasions, the difficulty of two
generations appreciating each other's point of view and
the practical problems of daily living—cleaning, cooking
and tidying—which are always increased by the presence
of children.

To promise love and loyalty to someone " for better
or for worse " until death is a brave declaration. Without
the sacrament of Matrimony it might well be a foolhardy
one, for love has so many enemies, the future is so
uncertain and even a long engagement can do little to
reveal the real character of another person. By the
sacrament of Matrimony, which each ministers to the
other, the human love of man and woman is made a
direct reflection of divine love. The married now love
each other, not merely with their own love but with God's
love " which knows no change nor shadow of alteration ".
It is in the strength of this love that they can face the
future so resolutely, can promise themselves to each other
so unhesitatingly; it is this love which gives them
the courage to endure all the difficulties that lie ahead

in the knowledge that, if they do not deliberately reject this love, it will carry them through life. " Jesus loved his own until the end ", St. John tells us, and it is in the power of his love that the married can love their own through all the vicissitudes and uncertainties of human life.

We have been looking at the seven sacraments in the light of the strength and hope they impart to human love, but we are not yet at the end of all that Christ has given us to enable love to gain its triumph. There is prayer, that gift of God by which we are able to articulate in our minds and hearts the unending prayer and dedication of Christ to his heavenly Father. In prayer we speak with no uncertain voice, for we speak with his voice; in prayer we are not attempting to bridge a vast abyss over which God lies distant, we are asserting that there is no such abyss and that God is with us and in us; in prayer we are not searching anxiously for God's presence and his gifts, we are triumphing in their possession. All prayer, because the prayer of Christ, is the prayer of love, and where love is, prayer cannot be distant. In all the difficulties of love's path we can turn to prayer for comfort, for light, for peace and for power. It is true that we cannot command the nature of God's response, for God alone knows what it is that love really requires; whether the apparent frustration of one love is not a necessary step to the fulfilment of another, whether we should not learn more about love if our selfishness is allowed to work love's death; whether we shall not in the long run rejoice in having undergone our present trials which have therefore in our own interests to be prolonged. We do not know the answer to any of these questions; but we do know that God never fails to hear the voice of his Son in " whom he is well pleased ". More powerful than resolution, more illuminating in its darkness than is reason in its light, prayer gives that peace which comes from the acceptance of things as they are and that promise for the future which the acceptance of the real present entails. Love is calling to love, light to light, life to life, and in the deep recesses of the human heart at prayer, life, light and love are mysteriously being renewed.

Finally, we are not alone. We are not alone either in love or in prayer, for we cannot be separated from that great array of created beings who live in and through Christ. We are living in him and they are living in him and therefore we are living in them and they are living in us. And if living, loving also. " Thousands upon thousands " in heaven have trodden the path of human love, have known its difficulties, and are sharing its triumph with us. In purgatory souls are resolving the difficulties of love in a different form of the same flame that is refining us. Those pure spirits, the angels, share with us a love whose intimacy and force we cannot even begin to conceive.

Above all the saints, towering over the angels, is the Queen of Heaven, the Mother of God. Never spotted by sin, never marred by selfishness, she loves her Son and all of us in her Son with a love past comprehension. Like all the truly innocent, she is full of sympathy with human frailty and we can always turn to her as to one who will understand what others fail to comprehend, who will believe in us when others no longer do so, who will measure us by our goodwill rather than by our failures. Her perfect love was tested by the utmost suffering that any purely mortal being could undergo and she will remain always close to human love, always ready to unravel the complexities which we bring to her to disentangle, always rejoicing in her title of " Mother of fair love ".

And above all, through all and in all is the Eternal Trinity; the root of being, the meaning of existence, the source and the object of love. In love it is, in love it creates, in love it acts. Co-eternal with existence, the source of our existence, the cause of creation, this love has been given to us so that beyond all the forms and symbols of a created universe our love shares in the infinite; victorious, it rises above time, place and circumstance back to its infinite and eternal source. In this ecstatic giving and receiving our love becomes certain, sure and fruitful. Certain, because it is not extinguished by time nor marred by events; sure, because it is independent of all that could halt its flight; and fruitful, because its fulfilment is inevitable and everlasting. Amid all the hesitancies of doubt, below all the pangs of jealousy, beyond all the promptings of selfishness, our love remains invincible. Outliving the sin that has warred against it, overcoming the selfishness that has marred it, transcending all the limitations that have made it seem precarious, love reigns triumphant from eternity to eternity. When faith has passed into sight and hope into realization, love remains. The end of ending and the death of death.

Nearly seven centuries ago, in her cell at Norwich

overlooking the crowded quaysides, the mudflats of the tidal river and the low wooded hills beyond, an anchoress summed up fifteen years of pondering upon God's revelations to her in these words: " And I saw that ere God made us he loved us: which love was never slacked, nor ever shall be. And in this love he hath done all his works; and in this love he hath made all things profitable to us; and in this love our life is everlasting. In our making we had beginning, but the love wherein he made us was in him from without beginning: in which love, we have our beginning. And all this shall we see in God without end." . . . " Then shall none of us be stirred to say in any wise: ' Lord, had it been thus, then it had been full well '; but we shall say all with one voice: ' Lord, blessed might thou be, for it is thus: it is well '."